SEWING, ETC.

Projects For All Seasons by Donna Salyers

Published by
Amanda Scott Publishing Company
Cincinnati, Ohio

DEAR READER

Each week for the past seven years I have written a newspaper column on sewing. When I began writing for my hometown paper, The Cincinnati Enquirer, I was terrified I would run out of ideas before the year's end.

That wasn't the case. My newspaper column is now syndicated throughout the country. I have a half-hour national cable television show each week. And I'm still finding interesting, even exciting, sewing projects.

For example, I never dreamed one could sew a down-filled coat until I discovered a mail-order resource for sewing kits called Altra, located in Boulder, Colorado.

After sewing my first down-filled vest, I was simply ecstatic! I could hardly wait to tell someone—anyone—that you really can sew something so inconceivable as a down-filled garment.

I didn't have a long wait. Indeed, I had only to sit down to my desk to write yet another sewing column.

This entire book is filled with projects that gave me a great deal of enjoyment and I'm thrilled to have the opportunity to share them with you.

I enjoy imagining how excited you'll be to discover, for instance, that there are alternative pattern sources for all sorts of specialty sewing (Spring, Not Your Everyday Pattern).

I know you'll really like the fabric-covered Parsons table (Spring, Parson Table Pointers). I remember completing my first table. I called my husband who was at work to see if he could come home to behold the sight!

After reading "Stitch A Swimsuit" in the Summer section, you have to try sewing a bathing suit! I was so pleased with my first bathing suit project that I promptly made four more. Why not? I had discovered a fabric store with a whole boxful of swimsuit panels selling for just $3 each.

I hope that you'll use this book, season by season, and that you'll find as much pleasure in sewing as I have.

ACKNOWLEDGMENTS

A special thank-you to:
my wonderful parents;
to Lynda Watcke, my sister and editor;
to Cindy Pratt, my sister and friend;
to Jack Klemack for his tenacity;
to my husband Jim and children, Amy and Scott,
for giving life meaning.

CONTENTS

CONTENTS (continued)

*Pattern on Master Sheet

WINTER

I love winter—especially in the heat of summer. Thoughts of a warm fire and the aroma of freshly baked bread are so appealing unaccompanied by the reality of the freezing cold.

Perhaps winter clothing is part of the appeal of the cold weather season. It's easier to get excited over gorgeous Ultrasuede® skirts and leather boots than chino pants and sandals.

In this section you'll find projects to keep you warm; to make you look good; and to give your home a sharp, custom look.

As for keeping warm, information on kits for sewing down-filled outerwear is contained in "Down-Filled Treasures". "Fun With Fur" will help you to sew a warm coat.

You don't know about log carriers? "Log Carrier Caper" tells how to get the logs from the woodpile to the fireplace without leaving a trail of debris in between.

When it comes to looking good, few things top an Ultrasuede® skirt or suit and a silky shirt. Personally, I prefer the wonderful immitation silkies because I can't stand ironing silk.

Ultrasuede® and similar luxury suedes are expensive, but I wear mine so many times that I can truly justify paying $50 or more per yard.

To illustrate: I had a lovely sand color Ultrasuede® skirt that I wore so many years it was becoming an embarrassment to my family and friends. When I couldn't bear to put it on one more time, I cut up the skirt and made a beautiful attache case.

Back to introducing Winter: "Opulent Ultrasuede®" and "Sewing Luxury Suedes" will help you to sew one ready knock 'em dead outfit.

For your home, you'll find instructions for making a table runner, Roman shades, and a braided holiday wreath.

SEWING A SILKY SHIRT

A silky classic shirt in creamy beige can become the foundation of a separates wardrobe. Wear it with a tweed skirt for work and with grey velvet trousers in the evening. A softly-gathered skirt of the same silky fabric will transform your shirt into a dress.

Shirt-making isn't all that difficult—there are fewer fitting problems in sewing a shirt than in sewing a pair of pants or a jacket. By virtue of size alone, a shirt can be sewn relatively quickly.

Perfect pockets and easy buttonbands will save you precious sewing time.

PERFECT POCKETS

The easiest pocket shape to work with has an angled base. While one pocket usually isn't a problem, making two identical, symmetrically shaped pockets is a different story. The following technique, however, should produce excellent results in no time.

•After narrow hemming, fuse interfacing to pocket facing for a crisp edge. Fold pocket facing to right side and machine stitch along seamlines only in the facing area. Trim seam allowance and turn facing.

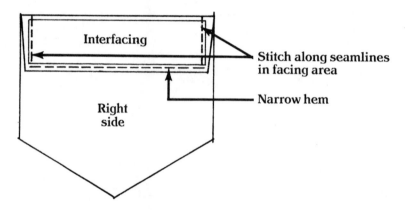

•Keep in mind that this next step will be done only once, and remember that the resulting template or pattern may be tucked into the pattern envelope and used many times over. It's best to make a template or pattern of heavy typing paper.

•This may be quickly done by placing the pattern tissue over carbon and heavy paper and precisely tracing the <u>finished</u> pocket shape. Cut out template.

•Place the right side of faced pocket against template with upper edges even. Pin in place.

•Using the template as a guide, fold and pin the pocket to conform to the shape of the template. If heavy paper was used, pins will penetrate the fabric only. Remove pocket from template, press, and remove pins. Topstitch pocket to shirt front.

EASY BUTTONBAND

A buttonband is an excellent detail, well worth the extra time it takes for topstitching. Even here, there's a shortcut:

•A separate pattern piece may be included for the buttonband. This shortcut, however, calls for cutting the shirt and band as one, eliminating the matching of plaids and prints, as well as simplifying pinning and cutting. (Use of this technique is limited to fabrics identical on front and back.)

•To cut a buttonband and front as one: Mark points $2\frac{1}{2}$ inches from the center front and connect with a straight edge. (See diagram.) This will be the new cutting line. The finished button-band will be $1\frac{1}{4}$ inches wide.

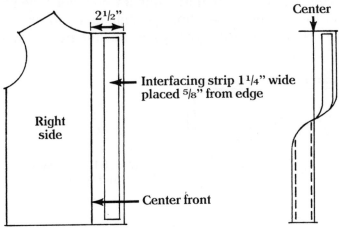

2¹/₂"

Center

Interfacing strip 1¹/₄" wide placed ⁵/₈" from edge

Right side

Center front

•If fusible interfacing is used, cut a strip the length of the shirt front and $1\frac{1}{4}$ inches wide. Fuse to the <u>right</u> side of the fabric, ⁵/₈ inch from the cut edge.

•Press under ⁵/₈ inch toward the interfacing. Turn and pin interfaced edge so that the wrong side is up, forming a $1\frac{1}{4}$ inch wide buttonband. Press in place and topstitch along edges of buttonband.

•If a non-fusible interfacing is used, for a fine silk-like fabric, for example, cut featherweight interfacing as above. Secure interfacing with a washable glue stick ⁵/₈ inch from fabric edge as above.

MAGIC YOKE

This yoke technique, borrowed from ready-to-wear, is a marvelously engineered method for stitching all the seams of a shirt yoke by machine.

This method is not only faster, but more attractive than the traditional hand-sewn method. All raw seam edges are completely encased without topstitching giving a fine look that is especially desirable on a silk or silk-like fabric.

You'll want to use this method any time a straight yoke is used. It is a technique difficult to visualize, however, so follow these instructions step-by-step:

•Cut two yokes, even if the pattern calls for one. For a heavy jacket fabric, for instance, use a lining weight fabric for the inside yoke. I'll call the outside layer "yoke" and the inside layer "lining".

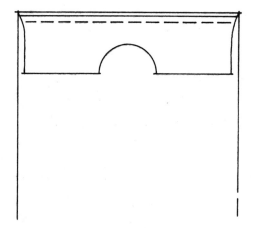

Sandwich back between lining and yoke

•Let's assume gathers are evenly distributed on shirt back and fronts, ready to attach to yoke. Before stitching, draw sewing guidelines 5/8 inch from the edge on the lining only.

•Pin and stitch wrong side of back to right side of lining.

•Pin yoke to back, right sides together, in essence sandwiching the back between the yoke and lining. Stitch with lining on top, following the first row of stitching.

•Trim seam allowance to 1/4 inch. Press yoke, lining, and seam allowances up away from shirt back.

•Pin and stitch wrong side of each front to right side of lining.

•Roll up fronts and back of garment and bring yoke and lining together, encasing garment. Stitch yoke to lining and front with lining on top, following the first row of stitching.

•Trim seam allowances and pull rolled up garment through neck. At this point you'll discover yoke is complete, with the inside looking as finished as the outside.

DOWN-FILLED TREASURES

Ski wear; so attractive and functional, is no longer just for the skier. But, alas, bona fide down-filled garments are expensive, largely because of the tremendous amount of labor involved. Eliminating labor costs could cut the price of a down-filled garment in half.

Altra Sewing Kits enable the home seamstress to do just that. Altra, a home-sewing mail-order firm based in Boulder, Colorado, offers the home seamstress the option of supplying the labor to produce a garment comparable to the finest ski wear available in ready-to-wear.

Altra, which in Italian means other or alternative, has kits for making vests, parkas, jackets, ski coveralls, even soft luggage and comforters. Most garments are available in unisex sizes to fit both children and adults in a variety of colors.

Each kit is complete in that it contains pre-cut fabric pieces, down plus the tools to insert it without mess, high-loft poly insulation, zippers, thread, and fasteners. Everything, including care, size, and manufacturer's labels, is included.

Altra promises instructions so explicit and simple that the first-time seamstress, can successfully complete an Altra kit. An executive I know who works for a Cincinnati fabric distributing company challenged this claim. Charlie had never sat down to a sewing machine before he made his down-filled ski vest.

By any standards Charlie's test garment would be considered advanced sewing: chevron quilted stripes for design interest, insulated pockets, inside pockets for carrying change or keys, an accessory ring to hold gloves or lift ticket, and separating zipper extending to a roll-up/down collar, plus optional zip on/off sleeves.

Said Charlie: "I can tell you a lot about a seam ripper. But my finished vest was perfect. It looked as good or better than the manufacturer's samples. It was fun; I found myself getting up at six in the morning to sew before I went to work. I enjoyed it so much I ordered two more kits to make up."

I tried my hand at a vest of about the same degree of difficulty as Charlie's. I cut his time in half, finishing in about twelve hours. It was a fascinating project, introducing completely new techniques and materials such as searing and handling down.

The amusing instructions were part of the fun: "Grit your teeth and stitch a second time," and "Pat yourself on the back and take a break." It was a bit like working a puzzle as the cut pieces from the kit looked like no shapes I've ever encountered in more than two decades of sewing. Yet by following the instructions precisely, everything fell nicely into place.

Whether or not you decide to sew a down-filled jacket, searing is a technique you'll find useful. We've all observed how the unfinished edges of a nylon parka can ravel to shreds in no time. Searing, a time-consuming process of using heat to melt the fabric edge to form a seal, will eliminate such raveling.

Altra recommends searing each cut edge before sewing by using the heat of a short candle such as one used with a food warmer, or a soldering iron. (Good grief!)

Undivided attention is essential, needless to say, to avoid torching the fabric. I chose a candle and dreaded even beginning, but was pleasantly surprised to find it an easy task after a few moments practice on the scrap supplied in the kit. I've become a pro since I made my first vest and people who compliment my homemade down-filled coats and soft luggage, are amazed to learn they are homemade.

To sear using an Altra kit, or any other nylon taffeta or nylon ripstop:

•Allow the rising heat, not the actual flame, to do the searing.

•Hold fabric tautly with both hands. With wrists resting on work surface, slowly move fabric edge past candle base.

•Searing, properly done, will be nearly invisible. The melted fibers form a fine ridge just on the fabric edge.

Altra kits are sold through fabric dealers or contact Altra directly for a catalog: Altra Sewing Kits, 5541 Central Avenue, Boulder, Colorado 80301 or call their toll free number: (800) 621-8103.

BREAD WARMER WINNERS

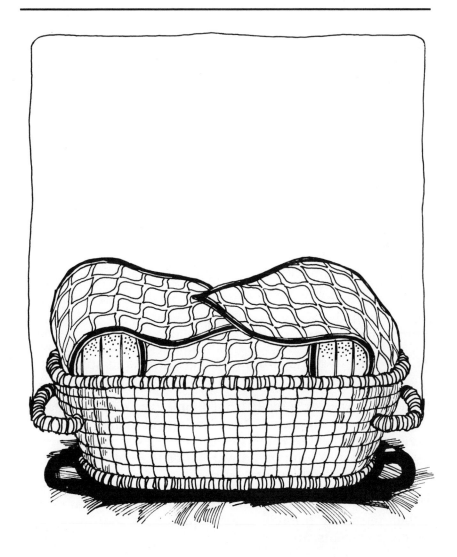

Many of the most beautiful and interesting of our American crafts originated from the people of the Appalachian Mountains. Cornhusk dolls, toys whittled from wood, and quilts made from scraps are all examples of a fundamental, make-something-from-nothing way of life.

The bread warmer sketched is such an item. Made from just a bit of fabric, these bread warmers sell for $15 in the student's workshop of Berea College in Berea, Kentucky.

Useful, pretty, and easy to sew, a bread warmer is the perfect fall project—just when you feel like baking bread (or at least buying some at the bakery).

FABRIC

One bread warmer requires two 18-inch squares of medium weight washable fabric, and if desired, 2 1/2 yards of trim.

The bread warmers sold at Berea College were made from two layers of natural colored linen and one flap was stamped with a potato print design. The basic design, however, lends itself to a wide range of fabrics—perhaps the very scraps in your fabric collection:

•Line blue denim with red gingham check after stitching red rickrack onto seam lines.

•Use a quilted eyelet with yellow gingham on the reverse side. Stitch a narrow eyelet ruffle in the seams.

•Cut a bread warmer from a holiday print and stitch a purchased applique such as a sprig of holly onto one flap.

•If a bread warmer is made from double-face quilted, only one layer of fabric is required. After cutting, all that remains to be done is to bind edges with wide bias tape. It's a great opportunity to add a matching bread warmer to the placemats you've made from quilted placemat fabric.

•Cut a bread warmer from white linen and pipe seams with either pastel or brightly colored piping to coordinate with china, placemats, and other linens.

•Linen is an excellent "canvas" for fabric painting. Plan a bread warmer around a painted motif or monogram.

HOW-TO

•For each bread warmer and using the pattern in the back of this book, cut two 18-inch squares with cutouts. If a double-face quilted square is used, cut only one thickness.

•Using a quarter-inch seam allowance, stitch cording, rick-rack, or narrow lace around the entire edge. This trim will not only add design interest, but will make it easier to open fabric edges after turning.

•Place the two shapes right sides together, aligning edges. No need to pin the entire edge, but simply pin randomly to keep fabric from shifting.

•Machine stitch around the entire edge, leaving a three-inch opening for turning. Keep stitching just inside the previous row of stitching used to secure trim.

•Turn bread warmer right side out and press edges flat. At this point you'll be happy you took the trouble to add the trim since smoothing edges flat and pinning inch by inch won't be necessary.

•Close opening with hand stitching. As an alternative you might insert a narrow strip of fusible web inside the opening and fuse with hot iron.

FUN WITH FUR

Is there a woman alive able to resist a fur coat? Well, yes—some for humanistic reasons, others due to concern for endangered species. Not to mention the initial expense and the ongoing maintenance a genuine fur requires.

Fake furs, on the other hand, offer a beautiful alternative. As a case in point, I made a "chinchilla" jacket. The cost of the jacket was approximately one-third the cost of a ready-made jacket. Though this particular fur must be dry-cleaned, many fake furs on the market may be machine washed and dried.

I used fur jacket pattern, Number 1015, from Stretch and Sew, cut specially for fur fabrics. This particular pattern is styled as a tailored coat with notched collar, side panels, and pockets set in the front side seams.

For all the style and detail, sewing moved quickly as the knit backing of the fur fabric permits quarter inch seam allowances which require no pressing or seam finishing.

If a fur jacket sounds a bit ambitious, bolster your confidence with a smaller project. Make a fur collar and cuffs for a coat already in your wardrobe. Lengthen a too-short coat with a fur border. Face a cape or coat with fake fur for a luxurious fur-lined look. Make a fur hat, muff, or stuffed toy. Just remember these guidelines:

•Place pattern pieces so that pile runs in the same direction. When working with a deep pile fur, nap should run downward. Cut single thickness. Place pattern pieces on the backing side and cut through backing only, not through pile. The backing is not "cut", but is snipped, using just the tip of the cutting shears, to avoid cutting through the pile on the right side.

•No getting around it, cutting is a messy job. So complete the cutting, take cut pieces outside, shake away loose pile, and then vacuum your work area. If a good quality fur cloth is used, there will be no shedding so the mess will be over at this point.

•Treat a fur as a plaid and lay pattern pieces so that shadings in the pile are properly spaced/matched when stitched together. The fabric I used, for example, is pearl grey with narrow lines of dark grey. In order to have a general idea of the location of the darker lines, I marked lines on the backing with straight pins and soap.

•Sewing texts generally say to stitch a conventional seam, and then advise using a straight pin to pull pile from seams. Stretch and Sew's method, however, streamlines the traditional method. Use a quarter inch seam allowance and stitch from bottom to top or against the nap. This method keeps fur from sliding on itself and seams practically disappear into the pile.

•Stitching very heavy fake fur may require machine adjustments. The most obvious adjustment will be to reduce presser foot pressure. Use a long stitch setting—about nine stitches per inch. Reduce upper thread tension, if necessary, to accommodate the bulk of the fur.

•For a classy closure, use fur hooks—the type used by furriers on fine genuine furs.

DECK THE HALLS WITH A HOLIDAY WREATH

You've heard about those old-fashioned Christmases—when decorations were handmade and each gift was a labor of love. People had more time than money and half the fun was in the preparation and anticipation of the holiday.

Perhaps you'd like to put a little tradition into your holiday by making a special decoration for your home and family. The wreath pictured is particularly nice because even small children can help—making it a family project.

You'll need three cuts of 45-inch fabric, each $^3/_8$ yards long; $1^1/_2$ pounds of poly fiberfill; and a big satin or velveteen bow.

The wreath consists of three poly-fill stuffed tubes, braided together. On the wreath pictured, I used three different calico prints with grounds of red, green, and yellow. Other soft, light-to medium-weight fabrics will work equally well:

•Gingham, perhaps in red and white of three different check sizes from tiny to very large.

•Velour or other plush fabrics in rich colors.

•Flannel in dark plaids.

Ready to start? It's easy—I promise:

•Use a yardstick and fabric marker or soap sliver to mark off $6^1/_4$ inch wide strips. Cut strips and stitch together to form three separate strips, each $6^1/_4$ inches wide and 65 inches long.

•Fold each strip in half, right sides together, and machine stitch on long edge, leaving ends open.

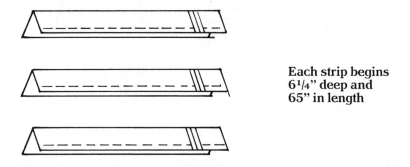

Each strip begins $6^1/_4$" deep and 65" in length

•Press open seam allowances with tip of iron. Turn each strip right side out.

•Stuff tubes from both ends with poly fiberfill, using a wooden spoon, pencil, or other long, narrow, blunt tool to push fiberfill towards center.

18

Tubes should be gently and lightly stuffed. To illustrate: my six-year-old son and I worked together. I, in typical adult fashion, tried to finish quickly, stuffing in big chunks of fiberfill, using adult strength.

My son, on the other hand, was having fun gently pushing in tiny pieces of fiberfill. Result: I had to use kitchen tongs to un-stuff a painfully bulging tube. Moral: sit by the fire and leisurely enjoy this family project.

•When stuffing is completed, close tube ends by machine, leaving a one-inch allowance at each end. Stitch the three tubes together by machine, first stitching two, then adding the third for ease in handling.

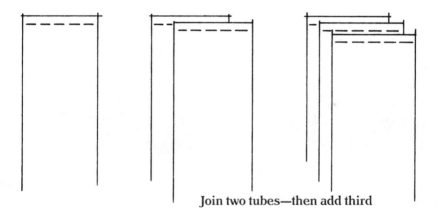

Join two tubes—then add third

•Practice braiding the wreath several times. After four or five attempts, you'll notice your work becomes more uniform. Shape and mold tubes with your hands to form a circular wreath. After final braiding, tubes will be uneven in length. Pin ends in position and secure with handstitching. Tie a beautiful velvet bow to cover the area where ends are joined.

LOG CARRIER CAPER

There's nothing like running outside in your bathrobe and socks to fetch an armload of wood for the fireplace and returning covered with bits of bark and grit, not to mention the trail of debris you brought in with you now decorating the carpet between the door and the fireplace.

A yard and a half of 50-inch denim and about an hour at the sewing machine will easily solve this problem. The solution is a log carrier, of course.

A log carrier is simply a rectangular piece of fabric with straps for carrying. Two or three logs are placed in the center and the straps are pulled up and around to cradle and carry the wood. When not in use, the log carrier can be folded and tucked away.

Begin with 1½ yards of 50-inch denim or canvas. On the selvage edges, cut two straps, each 5½ inches wide and 54 inches long. From the remaining 38-inch width of fabric, cut a rectangle 38 by 47 inches. (See diagram.) Half-inch seams are used throughout.

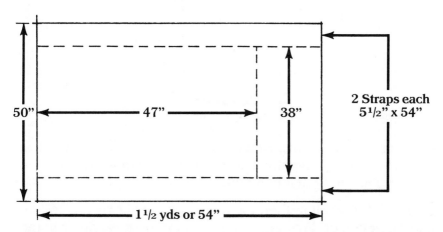

50"

47"

38"

2 Straps each
5½" x 54"

1½ yds or 54"

STRAP

Join ends of the two straps to form a circle. Turn ½ inch to wrong side along raw edge. Fold strap lengthwise so that selvage covers raw edge and strap is approximately 2½ inches wide. Topstitch along each edge twice.

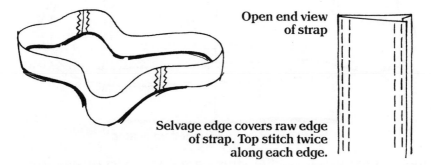

Open end view
of strap

Selvage edge covers raw edge
of strap. Top stitch twice
along each edge.

LOG CARRIER

Fold rectangle in half, right sides together. Be careful here as seam goes length of carrier. Before stitching, check to see that the length of this seam is about 37-38 inches.

Press seam open and, still with wrong side out, smooth carrier so that seam is centered. Stitch remaining ends, leaving a 4-inch opening at one end for turning.

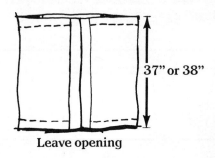

Leave opening

Clip corners and turn. Smooth and pin seam allowances in opening. There's no need to close this opening with hand stitching as the final topstitching will do the job.

Press both ends flat, then topstitch twice. Fold carrier in half and mark center. Position seams of strap on this center point.

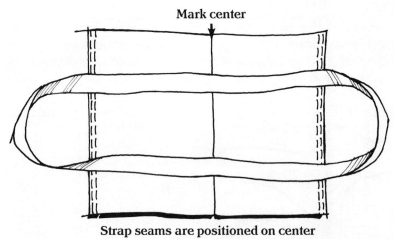

Strap seams are positioned on center

Pin strap to carrier so that straps are about 5 1/2 inches from each side. Stitch strap to carrier, following previous stitching on straps. Reinforce straps as illustrated.

If you prefer, three yards of heavy webbing may be used instead of the fabric strap.

SEWING LUXURY SUEDES

Entire books have been written on how to sew Ultrasuede®. In the space of a few pages, I won't pretend it is possible to tell you everything you'll want to know before cutting into your investment.

On the other hand...I can offer a few pointers:

• Don't pay $55 a yard or whatever is the going market price. There are mail-order sources which regularly discount Ultrasuede®. Imaginations, is one such resource. If you prefer to buy locally, watch for sales. Fabric distributors tell me 25%-off sales are not unusual.

• Consider alternatives to Ultrasuede®. Amara, for example, is a luxury suede cloth, similar in appearance to Ultrasuede®. The major difference is Amara is quite soft and pliable—more like real suede, while Ultrasuede® is somewhat stiffer.

From Pellon, Amara is 45 inches wide, as is Ultrasuede®; is priced in the same range as Ultrasuede®; is machine wash and dry. Amara is great for a belted jumper or dress, while the stiffness of Ultrasuede® makes it more suitable for belts, handbags, and other more structured items.

• Consult a good reference book on sewing luxury suedes, before purchasing your fabric. One such book is <u>Sew Smart</u> by Clotilde Yurick and Judy Lawrence. <u>Sew Smart</u> contains a complete section on sewing Ultrasuede® and similar luxury suedes. In addition, they offer another book entitled <u>Sew Smart With Ultrasuede® and Other Luxury Suedes</u>, which revises and expands the Ultrasuede®section contained in <u>Sew Smart</u>.

• Before making a luxury suede garment, shop ready-to-wear to see how experts handle luxury suede. Note colors—which may have an entirely different look made up in a garment as compared to indentical fabric on the bolt. Note choice of design and the various methods of seaming.

• Do try sewing one of the luxury suedes if you have had at least a little sewing experience. With the proper techniques, sewing luxury suedes is surprisingly easy. Begin with an eye glasses case, a belt, or a simple vest. A softly gathered skirt can be put together easily. A raglan sleeve jacket is a good second project.

•There's an economy in sewing luxury suedes, owing to lapped seaming and the fact that grain lines need not be strictly observed. Once seam allowances and hems are trimmed, the decrease in needed yardage is amazing. I made a blazer, from only 1½ yards of 45-inch Ultrasuede® and can make a softly gathered skirt from ¾ yard.

•You'll find many a how-to advising, "don't worry about topstitching—it just sort of disappears into the nap of the fabric." I strongly disagree, and feel the beauty of most suede garments is in well-done, even topstitching.

My Viking Sewing Machine has no trouble sewing a perfect, even stitch on Ultrasuede®. Before settling for topstitching which disappears into the fabric, experiment on scraps. Loosen thread tension; use a small needle (9 or 11) and a good quality thread. A Teflon-coated foot available through Viking dealers will reduce friction and aid in even stitching.

•Did you know there are many fabrics dyed to match Ultrasuede® including fine silky blouse and lining weights, corduroy, and even buttons?

•To contact Imaginations, call (617)620-1411; or write to 51 Marble at Blandin Avenue, Framingham, Mass. 01701.

•For order information on Sew Smart, write to Clotilde, 237 SW 28th Street, Ft. Lauderdale, Florida 33315

TEMPTING TABLE RUNNERS

Table runners are one of the most contemporary looks in linens today. Even if you're not crazy about sewing, but simply enjoy the end result—quick and easy-to-sew table runners, are for you.

Table shape and your own personal preference will dictate your needs:

•A long narrow table might have two runners placed length-wise. Or use two runners crosswise to seat four; center a third runner on the table length to seat six.

•A round or oblong table might have two runners placed at right angles.

•Top a tablecloth with a quilted runner to serve as decorative protection from hot dishes.

FABRIC

Single face quilteds, linen-like weaves, and decorator prints are excellent fabric options. Consider the less traditional fabrics too. Natural canvas, for example, trimmed with navy might better suit a summer picnic table or beach-front condominium. A contemporary glass and chrome decor might call for a taupe suede cloth.

Supply design interest with the use of contrast lining. For instance, back a beige and tan sea shell print with a coordinating solid tan. For a white linen-like fabric, use a self-lining and pale blue cording to accent fragile silver-trimmed china. For a country table setting, use a tiny navy/white provencial print, backed with navy and piped in red.

FIRST...SOME BASICS

•A finished table runner should be 12 to 15 inches wide, depending on table size. For good balance, the longer the table, the wider the runner should be.

•The drop, that is the length of fabric hanging over the table edge, should be 8 to 10 inches.

•Lengthen a panel from either end. For example, add two 12-inch lengths to a 24-inch panel to equal 48 inches rather than joining a 36-inch length and a 12-inch length.

SEWING

Many of us find it difficult to do an expert job of finishing an edge using the traditional satin stitch finish or double fold bias tape methods. If you're in the market for a fail-proof method, choose either of the following two methods.

Method One

For lightweight fabric where two thicknesses will be used, cord the seams. Use narrow seam allowances—about $1/4$ inch or whatever is the width of the cording seam allowance. Seams will need no trimming and the bonus will be fabric edges that pull out easily just by turning the runner and pushing the cording away from the seams with a steam iron.

For this method, cut runner to size, plus ½ inch longer and ½ inch wider. Be sure to round corners as the rounder the corners, the easier edges will turn.

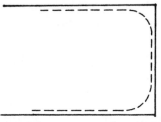

Round corners for ease in both stitching and turning

Step-by-Step: stitch cording to right side of one table runner. Place runners right sides together and pin. Stitch around entire runner, leaving an opening for turning. Stitch precisely on the first row of stitching. Turn runner and close opening with a strip of fusible web.

Method Two

For a heavy fabric such as canvas, a suede cloth, or decorator fabric requiring no lining: cut runner to size, adding 2½ inches to width and one inch to length for hemming.

Finish all raw edges with a three-step zig-zag (the selvage is a freebie). Or turn under each raw edge about ¼ inch and machine stitch. Fold a one-inch hem to wrong side along both long edges. Secure as follows:

•Simply machine topstitch—in this case straight stitching is essential. If your machine has no guide, place masking tape on machine bed to furnish a guideline against which fabric will be aligned during stitching.

•Or use a decorative machine stitch to secure hem. Use a contrasting or matching thread—contrasting thread if you are a straight stitching expert.

•Or, with hem pinned in place and working on the right side, add a trim such as soutache or wide bias tape. If trim is so wide that two rows of stitching are required, be sure to stitch each side in the same direction to avoid puckering and wrinkling.

Finish ends with a narrow hem.

ROMANTIC ROMAN SHADES

If you're thinking about new window coverings, you might consider roman shades. They have such a classy, custom look. Surprisingly, roman shades are simple to sew. Compared with pinch pleat draperies, roman shades use less than half the amount of fabric found in pinch pleat draperies for a similar size window.

A roman shade begins with a flat width of fabric which should be lined. To the flat fabric, tapes with evenly spaced rings are sewn. A light wooden slat is inserted in the hem at the base of the shade and the upper edge is stapled or tacked to another wooden slat for a clean, straight edge.

A cord is tied to the first ring in each row and runs up through the rings, through a screw eye, and across the top. For each row of rings, there is a separate cord. All the cords run across the top and to one side where they are tied off into one long cord. The shade is raised and lowered by that cord.

An awning cleat is mounted along side the window. When the cord is wound around the cleat, the shade is held in a raised position.

Shades made of brightly printed fabric and left untrimmed can be inexpensive. The use of elaborate trims, however, can make roman shades quite expensive.

Choose a light to medium weight decorator fabric. Do not choose an upholstery weight fabric. For the lining I prefer a white or beige flat bed sheet which won't require piecing and is much less expensive than buying fabric by the yard.

A shade might run from the ceiling to just below the window sill or might be the exact window size.

Whatever size you choose to make, purchase enough fabric to cover the area you desire plus two inches for side hems and seam allowances for joining panels. To the length, add eight inches for attaching at the top and for the lower casing.

If you plan to machine launder your shade, run all the uncut materials, including the ring tape, through a wash and dry cycle to prevent future shrinkage.

SEWING

•Seam together lengths of decorator fabric to make the outside layer of the shade. Center the largest panel.

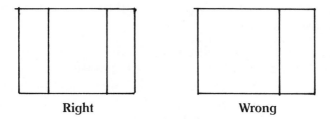

Right   Wrong

Seam panels in uniform segments

•Cut the lining sheet one inch narrower than the outer layer so that when the two are sewn together, using $1/2$ inch seam allowances, the seam will be on the underside and there will be no bulky seam allowances at the sides.

•Place the two fabric layers right sides together and pin and stitch along each side. Press the seams open and flat. Remember that the outer layer is larger than the lining, so center and smooth the lining under the outer layer. Machine stitch across the base of the shade.

•Turn the shade and pin edges so the lining doesn't shift. To simplify this, imagine that you've just stitched a pillow case that's closed on three sides.

•Place the shade on a flat surface, lining side up. With a yardstick and pencil or fabric marker, mark the tape positions. Tapes may be spaced eight to twelve inches apart and, of course, should be equally spaced.

Be very precise and accurate in drawing lines. Accuracy here means the shade will hang properly. Once the lines are drawn, pin the ring tape over the guidelines.

When positioning the tape the position of the first ring in each line must be uniform in distance from the base of the shade. For example, the first ring in each row might be four inches from the base so there will be room for a casing to hold the slat.

•Use a zipper foot in stitching the tape to the shade, keeping the tape centered over the guideline. It is sometimes suggested that tapes be secured with two rows of stitching, one along each edge. I prefer to use just one row so that stitching will be less conspicuous on the completed shade.

•After securing tapes, turn up the base about 1 1/2 inches and machine stitch to form a casing to contain the wooden slat.

•If a shaped hem is desired, seam together widths of fabric same as shade. The decorator fabric of the hem panel might be interfaced. After fusing interfacing, place decorator fabric and lining right sides together and stitch side seams. Press seams open and flat. Place panel on flat surface and use a yardstick and fabric marker to draw hem shape. Here again, planning is most important as scallops, dentils (squares), or whatever must be centered.

•Machine stitch shaped hem. Clip curves, turn, and press. Sew panel to shade just above casing stitches.

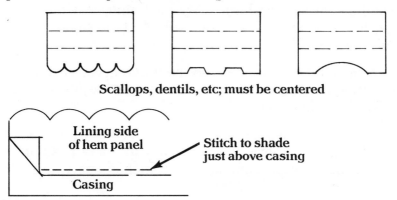

Scallops, dentils, etc; must be centered

Lining side
of hem panel

Stitch to shade
just above casing

Casing

INSTALLATION

•Staple or tack upper edge of shade to support slat. Nail slat in position above window from underneath shade so that raw edge of shade is against wall.

•Insert screw eyes in window frame precisely in alignment with ring tapes. Cut lengths of nylon cord, each of which will be a different length, to tie to bottom ring, run up through rings on tape, through eyes, and down to form a shade pull.

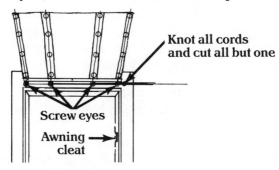

Knot all cords
and cut all but one

Screw eyes

Awning →
cleat

•While shade is hanging in extended position, tie all cords together and cut all but one cord length.

•Raise shade to desired height and wrap cord around cleat mounted along side the window. Retie cords to bottom rings, if necessary, to assure shade hangs evenly.

OPULENT ULTRASUEDE®

A glasses case makes a great stocking stuffer. Use this basic how-to, then have fun creating your own designs with contrasting trim, quilting, or decorative stitching.

Use Ultrasuede® scraps, or if you have no scraps on hand, one-eighth yard of Ultrasuede® will make three cases. Lining fabric is needed, but the lining will be barely visible, so don't worry if yours is not a perfect match. Use a medium-weight fusible interfacing.

•Using the glasses case pattern, found at the back of this book, cut two rectangles of Ultrasuede, two linings, and two interfacings.

     2 Ultrasuedes®   **2 linings**   **2 interfacings**

•Trim away a half-inch from each edge of the interfacings. Trim about a half-inch from the sides only of the linings.

•Center interfacing on wrong side of Ultrasuede® and fuse in place.

•Press under one-half inch on upper edge of each lining piece. With wrong sides together, place lining on Ultrasuede close to upper edge. Secure with narrow strip of fusible web (such as Magic Polyweb), double face tape, or glue stick.

Glue lining to wrong side of Ultrasuede® after stitching

Lining

Outside

Use glue stick or fusible web to hold lined halves together

•Topstitch across top to permanently secure lining. Use two rows of topstitching, the first row close to fabric edge, the second row about three-eighths inch from edge. Secure lining in lower area with glue stick. To join halves, place linings together and secure Ultrasuede® with fusible web or glue stick.

•Topstitch about one-fourth inch from the edge around three sides of the case. With sharp scissors and a sure, steady stroke, trim Ultrasuede® close to stitching for a clean, finished edge.

•Topstitch a second time about three-eighths inch from the fabric edge.

Though case is complete at this point, you may wish to:

•Add a button tab when joining lining to Ultrasuede.®

•Center a strip of Ultrasuede® on one side after applying interfacing.

•Add a monogram if you're adept at machine embroidery.

•Create an interesting pattern with rows of twin-needle stitching.

•Join halves together with decorative machine stitching.

SPRING

The feedback I receive from newspaper readers and TV viewers is always of great interest to me. I know how impassioned I must be to take time to write a letter to an editor or an entertainer.

I read mail and take calls with the belief that those who take time to contact me are equally emphatic about their opinions.

Sensitive as I am, it's fortunate for me that people usually write to sewing columnists only to express pleasure in something.

What all this has to do with introducing the Spring section are two responses I recently received.

A few years ago in my syndicated newspaper column I wrote about sewing a Bermuda bag and told how to draft a pattern. Not long ago I heard from a young mother of three children whose husband had been out of work for nearly two years.

During that period, this ingenious woman had supported her family by sewing and selling Bermuda bag covers. She had used the instructions which had appeared in my column.

At first, she sold the covers to friends and neighbors. At one point she took the covers she had sewn to a department store where she was told her work wasn't up to their standards.

She continued sewing and selling her Bermuda bag covers to individuals and at craft fairs. Six months later she went back to the department store and made a deal to supply them with covers for the entire spring and summer seasons.

While I wot't mention her name, I salute her and others who don't give up. We all find ourselves in trying circumstances at one time or another. If this happens to be one of those difficult times for you, I hope that something so inconsequential as a pattern for a Bermuda bag cover comes along to help you turn things around.

My second anecdote isn't so heartwarming, but made me feel wonderful nonetheless. When I began my television show Sewing, Etc., I was even more terrified than when I began writing a newspaper column.

It's one thing to write a newspaper column in the comfort of your own furnace room (which doubled as my office). I could write, rewrite, then rewrite my rewrite before turning it in.

Going into a TV studio is something else again. Should one really have to learn how to do a TV show before a national audience? Thanks to lots of wonderful backup support, I made it through.

I'll never forget when our first Nielsen rating came in. It was a hot summer afternoon and after a long day at work, I was unwinding by cutting the grass. My son Scott came running out to tell me I had a long distance phone call.

It was Charlie Murdock, an innovative and courageous pioneer in cable TV who founded the production company which produces my show along with several others.

Charlie was ecstatic! The Nielsen ratings proved our show was a success.

Oh incidentally, Charlie had run in to an executive at CBN who had seen me on Sewing, Etc., covering a plastic Parsons table with fabric. This gentlemen liked the idea so much he had gone home that evening and covered a table with fabric.

I hope you think the "Parsons Table Pointers" in this section is a good idea too.

When you read "Elegant Evening Bags", remember a pattern is included at the back of this book. The prettiest bag I've made is lavendar velvet with a silver rope handle, and trimmed with silver metallic ribbon.

If you enjoy trivia, be sure to read "Timely Tapunto Tips". What ever is trapunto? It's a quilting technique which you've probably seen many times but just didn't know it by name.

BERMUDA BAG BEAUTIES

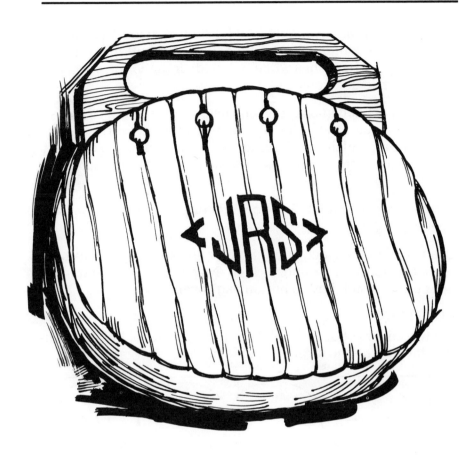

A Bermuda or button bag is one of my favoite sewing projects. Never out of style, these bags can be found in all types of fabric from linen with hand-painted butterflies, to madras patchwork, to cotton poplin with a monogram.

Spend $10 to $20 for a Bermuda bag cover, depending on the amount of custom work desired, or make one from a 3/8 yard remnant. Because so little fabric is required, perhaps you'll find just the perfect piece of quilted fabric in your scrap collection, Or, choose a fine embroidered cotton which, in a larger quantity, might be unaffordable. Since you're working on a small scale, it's an excellent opportunity to experiment with machine embroidery, quilting, applique,' or fabric painting.

Bermuda bags are available in at least three sizes. Use the pattern at the back of this book which fits a four-button frame and measures 8 x 10 inches when finished, or grade the pattern to fit your particular frame.

The cover is lined and corded and uses only two pattern pieces: an egg-shaped cover plus a center strip. One fabric may be used for both outside and lining; or line a print with a contrasting solid to create design interest and to utilize small scraps as well.

For cording seams, about two yards of piping or rickrack are needed.

Use a seam allowance equal to the allowance of the piping—probably between $1/4$ and $1/2$ inch. Now get to work and in an hour or two you'll have a button bag cover.

CUTTING

Cut two covers of outside fabric; cut two covers of lining or outside fabric; cut one strip of outside fabric.

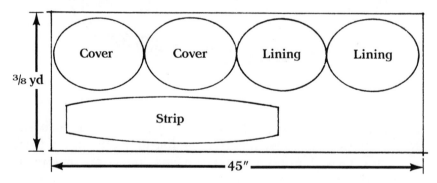

•Optional: fuse a strip of interfacing along the upper edge of each lining cover to stabilize buttonhole area.

SEWING

Using a zipper foot, stitch piping or rickrack on right side around entire edge of two outside covers.

•With right sides together, pin piped cover to lining, matching notches and pinning randomly. Repeat for other side of cover.

•Using a zipper foot, stitch between the two upper notches only. Stitching should be just inside the first line of stitching which secured piping. Repeat for other side of cover.

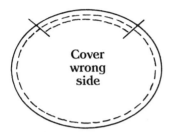

Stitch two covers together, stitching between notches only

•Clip notches to stitching line and turn each cover right side out. Pin cover and lining randomly, aligning edges. Machine stitch lower edge of cover/lining together, stitching precisely on piping stitch line. This step may seem unnecessary, but will furnish a stitching guideline for attaching the center strip. Repeat for remaining cover/lining.

•Cover at this point might be monogrammed, appliqued, or personalized in whatever style suits you and your fabric. I've had great success using acrylic paints to add a monogram and floral motif.

•With right sides together, pin strip to one cover/lining, matching notches and allowing strip ends to remain free. Stitch around lower edge of cover, stitching from notch to notch, keeping stitches just inside previous line of stitching. Attach remaining cover/lining in a similar fashion.

•Fold strip ends to inside and secure with hand stitching.

•Place pattern over completed cover, marking placement of buttonholes. Make buttonholes.

TEE TIME GOLF SKIRT

That $30 golf skirt hanging in the pro shop, with no zipper and an elasticized waist, can be duplicated for about 20% of its retail price.

This project moves quickly as there is no zipper, buttonholes, or facings with which to contend. Add purchased straight-leg panties to sew to the waist, and you have an almost instant golf skirt.

Begin with a favorite A-line skirt pattern. Don't worry if there are darts and a zipper; they'll be eliminated in sewing.

Choose a light-weight, double-knit fabric; wovens will not work using this construction method. A surprisingly small amount of fabric is needed—only 5/8 yard of 60 inch fabric for mine. Be sure to measure your pattern before shopping.

Besides fabric and thread, you'll need one-inch wide elastic cut to waistline measurement and a pair of straight-leg panties purchased a size or two larger than your usual size.

CUTTING

Cut A-line skirt pattern as usual, ignoring darts and zipper markings. On cross grain, cut waistband to measurement of skirt waistline, plus seam allowances. The width of the waistband should measure 3 ¼ inches wide.

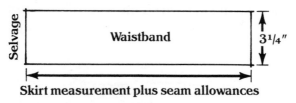

SEWING

Trim waistline elastic from panties. Stitch and press open skirt seams. With skirt right side out, slip panties inside. Right side of panties will be against wrong side of skirt.

Match and pin center and side seams of skirt and panties. Zigzag along upper edge, stretching skirt to fit panties.

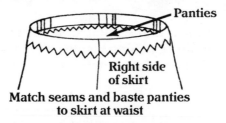

Close waistband. With right sides together, pin waistband to skirt, positioning waistband seam at side. Machine stitch ⅝ inch from edge, gently stretching both layers as you stitch.

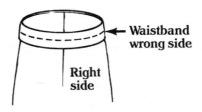

Using one-inch wide elastic, cut elastic about one inch smaller than waist measurement. Lap elastic ends and stitch to form a circle. Mark quarter points on elastic with pins. The center and side seams on skirt will furnish quarter points. If skirt has no center seams, however, determine centers back and front and mark at this time.

Position elastic on seam allowance so that quarter points match. Elastic will be smaller than skirt and must be stretched to fit. Using a medium zigzag stitch, stitch elastic to seam allowance. Stitch with elastic on top and slightly away from waistband stitching.

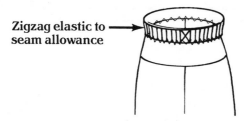

Zigzag elastic to seam allowance

Smooth waistband over elastic and fold to inside of skirt. Take care to pull waistband snugly over elastic so there is no unnecessary fullness.

On right side, stitch in the ditch; that is, machine stitch in the waistband seamline catching inside layer of waistband. Stretch waistband and skirt while stitching. Trim waistband close to stitching.

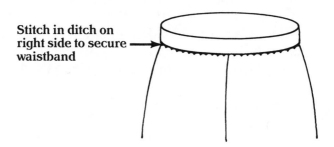

Stitch in ditch on right side to secure waistband

Hem skirt and you're all finished.

VARITIONS

It's fun to be creative and give your skirt your own personal style. Need a few ideas?

•Some of the most attractive golf skirts have narrow belts and belt loops. If you plan to add belt loops, pin loops in position and sew on at the same time the waistband is attached.

•Pockets can be functional as well as furnish design interest. Cut pockets into side seams or simply add patch pockets.

•Veteran golfers have, no doubt, seen some of the clever applique'work on the very expensive skirts. Applique'takes more time than money. The addition of a simple motif can create not merely a golf skirt, but a boutique item.

TIMELY TRAPUNTO TIPS

Trapunto...we see examples every day of this ancient quilting art, unaware perhaps of the technique, its name, or origin.

Trapunto is found in boutiques where satin, suede, and Ultrasuede® vests and jackets are embroidered and padded. A simpler form of trapunto is seen when an applique´is stitched to a pair of jeans and stuffed with poly-fill before stitching is completed.

Another form of trapunto called Italian quilting is used on sofa cushions where a raised design is created by drawing cord through stitched channels.

Historians believe quilting dates back as far as 3,000 B.C., evidenced by ancient statuary found in the Far and Middle East, showing quilted garments and robes.

Quilting, it is assumed, began out of necessity—for warmth—and later was used for protection as its use spread to Europe in the form of heavily padded and quilted armor.

Quilted covers and garments were naturally a status symbol among the very wealthy, and as the craft reached the warmer Southern European countries, a new form of raised quilting evolved. Called trapunto, this form of quilting encouraged the use of quilting as a means of decoration rather than a means of keeping warm.

All of which brings us to the subject of this chapter: trapunto—a quilting technique where a design is stitched through two layers of fabric. The bottom layer (backing) is slit and padding is inserted to raise the design.

I know of stitchery artists who have done trapunto just as craftsmen did long ago, using hand stitches to outline a design. Though this sounds like a form of slow torture to me, hand-worked trapunto might be just the craft that appeals to you. I, however, prefer to bring this ancient craft to the 20th Century by combining the use of a sewing machine with the marvelous graphic textiles available within the past few years.

The wallhanging pictured is an excellent vehicle for trapunto, as is the seashell pillow cover. On the other hand, many trapuntoed garments have a homemade look because the padding somewhat distorts the garment shape. A wallhanging or pillow cover, however, can be stretched back to its original form.

For machine trapunto, two layers of fabric are needed. The outside layer of fabric might be a graphic textile. Or choose a lightweight printed fabric such as a large floral print, a juvenile animal print, or a bold contemporary pattern.

The backing is a layer of lightweight (not knit) fabric, cut to the size of the outside layer. An old sheet or tablecloth will work nicely.

For padding, use poly fiber-fill sold in pound bags (or give a home finally to those wads of cotton found stuffed in vitamin jars).

Pin the backing layer to the wrong side of the outside layer. No need to baste, pinning is sufficient. With outside layer up, machine stitch around whichever parts of the design you wish to raise. There is no right or wrong way, just your personal preference. It's my experience, however, that random outlining is not only visually appealing, but creates less distortion and makes it easier to stretch the completed panel.

Upon completion of outline stitching, turn backing side up. Carefully snip holes in backing in area to be raised, taking care not to cut through the outside fabric layer. Push fiber-fill through slits, using the eraser end of a pencil or crochet needle to reach small areas.

It's unnecessary to close the slits on a wallhanging. For a pillow cover, however, simply handstitch the slit edges together.

For optimal results, keep in mind the following suggestions:

•Work on a large scale. Stuffing tiny little flower stamens and bird beaks in not conducive to good mental health.

•Choose light-colored fabrics. Trapunto depends on shadows and shadings created by the raised design, which will be lost on a darker color.

•Satins, cottons, velveteen and other even-textured fabrics are ideal for trapunto. Twill weaves, corduroy, burlap, and other fabrics of obvious texture will detract from the design.

•A lightweight knit or woven fabric will have enough give to raise when stuffed, while a heavy, tightly-woven fabric will not have sufficient elasticity to be effectively raised.

•Stuff lightly so that the overall shape of the pillow or wallhanging is not distorted.

ELEGANT EVENING BAGS

How frustrating to discover an evening bag in ready-to-wear costing as much or more than the fabric used to make a party dress. The evening bag described here can be made from a remnant, or you may want to splurge on a luxury fabric because the bag and lining require only one-fourth yard of 45-inch fabric.

The finished bag is 6¹/₂ inches wide, seven inches deep, and has a shoulder strap. Narrow embroidered trim, ribbon, or lace sewn to fabric backed with fleece will give the bag a quilted look.

If the bag is made of a lightweight fabric such as satin, both the cover and lining may be cut from the same one-fourth yard of fabric. If a velvet or tapestry is used, an additional one-fourth yard of lining is required. Three and one-half yards of embroidered trim is needed. Two yards of the trim are for a shoulder strap.

Use the 18 by 8 inch rectangular pattern found in the back of this book to cut one cover, one lining, and one layer of fleece. (Pellon fleece is a lightweight loft, sold where interfacing is stocked, and is used for quilting, shoulder pads, and the like.)

Draw trim guidelines on the right side of bag cover, using soap or fabric marker and ruler. The distance between lines will depend on trim width. For half-inch wide trim, for example, center first line, then draw a line two inches away on either side of center.

Pin fleece to wrong side of cover, keeping pins on right side. Center embroidered trim or lace on lines and machine stitch. Most trims will require two rows of stitching rather than a single row of stitching down the center. Slightly reduce upper machine tension to compensate for batting, and stitch in the same direction to avoid puckering.

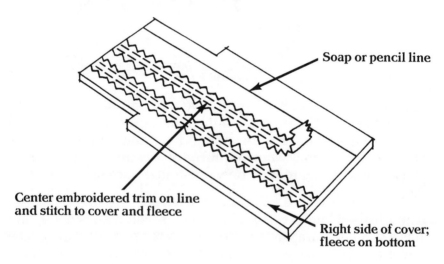

Soap or pencil line

Center embroidered trim on line and stitch to cover and fleece

Right side of cover; fleece on bottom

After applying trim, pin bag cover to lining, right sides together. Stitch around all sides, using a quarter inch seam allowance, but leaving a four-inch opening for turning as diagram indicates.

Trim seam allowances and clip angles to stitching.

Turn bag and close opening with hand stitching (or glue stick if your date is at the door).

To form bag, fold over lower half, right sides together, so bag is six inches deep. Machine stitch along sides using one-fourth inch seam allowances.

Make shoulder strap by stitching together two one-yard lengths of embroidered trim, right sides out. Or make a strap of satin or velvet cording, or from self fabric.

Secure strap to seam allowances inside bag. For flap closure use: Velcro fastener, a large covered snap, or an ornament or heavy bangle stitched to flap for weight.

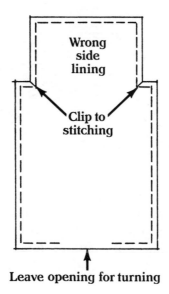

Leave opening for turning

DIRECTOR CHAIR DRAMA

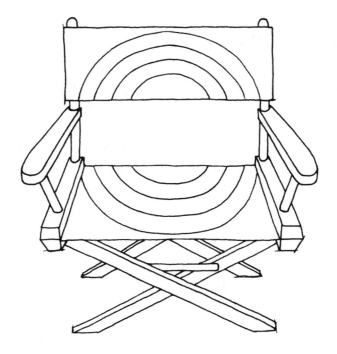

A few months of sun on a patio or boat can make director chair covers a bit weary for the wear. While replacement covers can be purchased, it's fun to make them yourself in just the color and design you wish—not to mention the fact that you'll save about two-thirds the cost of ready-made ones by doing it yourself.

Though you may find a limited selection of canvas in a fabric shop, your best bet is an awning and tent shop, where you'll find 18 ounce (the ideal weight) canvas in a wide range of colors.

Covers should be snug and about 3/4 inch narrower in width than the measurement of the chair frame. Use your old cover as a pattern, keeping in mind it may be stretched from wear.

HOW-TO

The layout for two covers cut from 35-inch wide canvas is dia-grammed.

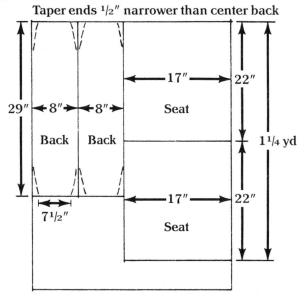

Taper ends ¹/₂″ narrower than center back

Single thickness 35″ layout for two chairs

•Use a yardstick and fabric marker or soap to draw cutting lines directly on canvas. Allow an inch for each hem turn-up as canvas is heavy and doesn't fold easily. When possible, use selvage edges to your advantage—they'll need to be turned only once instead of twice.

•Canvas is too heavy to fold and pin, so simply turn edges as you sew. To keep a uniform fold, draw a guideline one inch from edge and keep folded edge even with this line.

•Taper back so ends aren't visible on finished cover.

•I used ordinary sewing thread, simply because it was on hand. Had it not been after midnight, I'd have bought a heavy-duty thread. Two years later, however, stitches are holding just fine.

•In duplicating my old covers, I found a raw edge left on the channel or casing where dowels are inserted. It's a good idea to coat this edge with "Fray Check" to prevent raveling.

With covers complete, it's your turn to be creative by adding just the right touch of color or texture to accent your home:

• Use acrylic paint to write a name or title across the back. The name might be a large signature or stenciled letters.

• Add accent colors to solid color canvas by stitching bias tape in interesting designs.

• Stitch purchased woven trim to canvas covers, mitering corners.

• Create a pattern or give continuity to a decorating motif with machine sewn appliqués.

MIND OVER MENDING

You've faced the cold hard truth: you hate to sew. And the only reason you have your nose in a sewing book is: a) Your husband, still believing that one day he'll look in the closet and find a shirt with all its buttons, bought you this book; or b) Your aunt, who has always confused you with your sister, the Home Ec teacher, sent it to you.

Unless you are fortunate enough to have a maid on your premises replacing buttons, repairing hems, and mending small tears, mending can be avoided for only so long. So read quickly and I'll briefly highlight the abc's of mending.

Start with a few basic tools: scissors, tape measure, a six-inch sewing guage, a box of straight pins, a package of needles, thread in black, white, red, plus dental floss (hang in there, you'll see), one yard of fusible web, and a package of iron-on patches.

Be a saver. Before discarding a worn shirt, remove buttons and keep them on hand for replacements. Keep an old pair of jeans from which to cut patches to bond to the inside of still good, but torn jeans.

ABOUT BUTTONS
A button must have a shank, that is a thread "stem" between the button and the fabric, which will keep the button standing nicely on the bottonhole, rather than holding the buttonhole open, creating an unsightly gape. The heavier the fabric, the longer the shank. To the uninformed, however, a button on a long shank, necessary on a thick, heavy woolen coat, might be mistaken for a loose button.

Some buttons have a built-in shank—such as the type with a metal eyelet mounted on the back. A flat button for a shirt will need a thread shank which is created when the button is attached.

To replace a button, fasten surrounding buttons, snaps, hooks, or zippers. For a horizontal buttonhole, mark the button position with a pencil dot or a straight pin at the end of the buttonhole closest to the garment edge. For a vertical buttonhole, mark the position at the top of the buttonhole.

Horizontal buttonhole—button is placed closest to garment edge

Vertical buttonhole—button is placed at top of buttonhole

Or easiest of all, if a bit of thread or the needle holes remain from the original button, use them as a positon guide.

To replace a flat button, insert the threaded needle from the right side of the garment; the button will cover the knotted thread end for a neater job.

Bring the needle back up to the right side as close as possible to the knot. Insert needle through button. To create the shank, simply place a toothpick or match on top of the button while it is being stitched to the fabric.

Insert the needle through the second hole of the button and through fabric. Bring needle up through the first hole again, repeating this stitch about six times for a two-hole button. For a four-hole button, repeat the stitch about four times on each pair of holes.

The last stitch comes up through the garment, but not through the button. Remove the toothpick and hold button so stitches are taut. Wrap thread several times around stitches, which now have formed a shank. Insert needle through shank and knot thread as close to shank as possible. Clip thread close to knot—all done.

For a button with a metal eyelet: Insert the needle from the right side. Bring the needle back up to the right side, close to the knot. Insert the needle through the metal eyelet of the button. Stitch seven or eight times with each stitch going through the fabric as well as the eyelet. To finish, insert the needle through the stitches, knot thread, and clip thread close to the knot.

No matching thread? Thread the needle with dental floss. (You knew you'd finally use it for something.) Dental floss is extra strong and will adapt to the color of the garment.

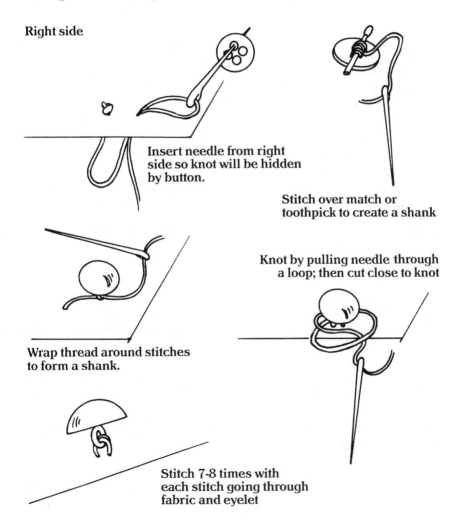

Right side

Insert needle from right side so knot will be hidden by button.

Stitch over match or toothpick to create a shank

Knot by pulling needle through a loop; then cut close to knot

Wrap thread around stitches to form a shank.

Stitch 7-8 times with each stitch going through fabric and eyelet

TEARS, PATCHES, HEMS

Sewing has changed dramatically in the past few years. Much of ready-to-wear is not sewn together, but is glued together. Actually the term is fused, and if fusing works in ready-to-wear, it will work for you also.

Stitch Witchery is but one of many fusing agents on the sewing market, available in narrow rolls or by-the-yard in 18-inch widths. When this white, translucent fusing material is placed between two thicknesses of fabric, and moist heat is applied (via a steam iron), the fusing agent melts, and two fabric layers are bonded together.

Iron-on patches work in much the same way as Stitch Witchery and are sold in packages at supermarkets, drug stores, and fabric stores.

Armed with Stitch Witchery, iron-on patches, and a steam iron, one may: bond a patch on the wrong side to keep knees, elbows, or other friction points from wearing; mend square tears or small holes; attach a decorative patch or applique´ (which might be covering a tear); or repair a hem.

FRAYED ENDS?

Dritz Fray Check is another type of bonding agent. A clear liquid packaged in a plastic squeeze bottle, Fray Check provides an invisible silicone coating which does not wash away.

A minute amount of Fray Check applied from the applicator tip to a fraying collar or cuff, will seal the fraying threads. This product can be used as a precautionary measure on new garments as well.

Fray Check has many additional uses: apply to fraying drawstrings on a parka or sweatshirt; seal fraying shoestring tips; stop the raveling of a jacket lining or collar point where seam allowances were trimmed too closely; or seal the raveling at the top of a zipper tape.

RACQUET COVERS ANYONE?

Garments and accessories found in tennis pro shops are always attractive and appealing. And well they might be—most are premium priced because such shops usually deal in low volume.

At a tennis pro shop not far from home, I discovered a terrific collection of racquet covers. Each racquet cover was priced at around $20. A unique treatment such as hand-painted stylized flowers, an appliqued tennis motif, or a monogram made each one special.

I could hardly wait to make one naturally, and hope this is an item which will appeal to you also. This is an especially good sewing project for beginners because it's quick and allows little time for frustration.

FABRIC
Choose a tightly woven, medium-weight fabric. Make it fun by shopping for a clever tennis print. Or you may wish to create design interest yourself, using brightly-colored letters to spell out a title or name on a solid color poplin.

Estimate fabric requirement after making the pattern described below. Purchase piping to set in the seam that encircles the cover.

PATTERN
Make a pattern by centering racquet head on a folded newspaper section. Trace, then redraw a cutting line to make pattern about one inch larger all around.

Trace racquet
on newspaper

Enlarge pattern
about 1″ all around

CUTTING
Use opened out pattern to cut one front. To cut back, fold pattern in half and position ⅝ inch from the edge on a double thickness of fabric to furnish seam allowances for zipper insertion.

SEWING
Complete the applique or monogramming work while front is flat. Make your own letters and appliques from a commercial applique pattern or use purchased iron-on calico letters.

If your fabric/trim combination is interesting, appliqués or additional trimming may not be necessary. For instance, a green and red tennis print on a white ground, piped in green, probably need not be enhanced with additional trim.

•Apply piping to right side of front using a zipper foot. Use a quarter-inch seam allowance, keeping raw edge of piping even with cover edge. (Jumbo rickrack or eyelet ruffling might be substituted.)

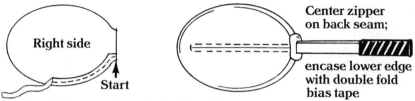

Right side

Start

Center zipper
on back seam;

encase lower edge
with double fold
bias tape

Apply cording or trim to right side of front

•Zipper begins one inch below the upper edge of cover back. Purchase zipper an inch or two longer than necessary. Allow excess tape to extend beyond base of cover where zipper pull is out of the way and won't interfere with straight stitching.

•Close back cover seam, using short stitches above zipper opening and long basting stitches in zipper area. Reinforce point just above where zipper begins by back-stitching twice before increasing stitch length. Press seam open. With soap or fabric marker and ruler, draw a stitching guide ³/₈ inch from either side of the seam on the right side.

•Working on wrong side, center closed zipper face down on seam. Secure each side of zipper tape with glue stick.

•Stitch zipper to cover, beginning at base of cover, up one side of zipper, across, and down remaining side.

•Remove basting in zipper seam. Pin front and back, right sides together. Still using a zipper foot, with front next to machine needle, stitch covers together, keeping edges aligned. Keep stitching just inside the row of stitching which secured piping.

•Encase the lower edge of the cover with double-fold bias tape.

NOT YOUR EVERYDAY PATTERN

Even with the tremendous number of patterns available through the Big Four pattern makers—Butterick/Vogue, McCall's, and Simplicity—sometimes our sewing needs are so unique that it's necessary to ferret out a special pattern resource.

Many of the contacts listed below took years of searching to discover, so I'm delighted to have an opportunity to share my finds. Because inventories and prices are subject to change, specifics have not been given. It is suggested that you write for a catalog or price list before ordering.

PETRONELLA PATTERNS, 1672 Donelwal Drive, Lexington, Kentucky 40511. The specialty here is patterns for making soft dolls. Owner and founder Mary Pat Warren's special interest is dolls—she's a collector. A brood of six athletic children plus their unending supply of worn tube socks made the business of designing dolls a natural for Warren.

These unusual patterns are for the needleworker who demands quality designs, but may have limited sewing ability.

Discarded tube socks furnish the basic form of each doll; discarded plastic lids give hands and feet their lasting shape. A packet of appropriately colored dye is included with each pattern. Because dolls are approximately 22 inches high, clothing can be sewn from scrap fabric.

PAST PATTERNS REPLICAS, 2017 Eastern S.E., Grand Rapids, Michigan 49507. This one-woman operation specializes in authentic patterns of vintage clothing, chiefly from the 1890's and the early 1900's. Saundra Altman, owner of this mail-order business, seeks out very special designs to duplicate—not just everyday clothing of a period.

These patterns are of special interest to brides, antique automobile collectors, equestrian groups and historical preservation groups. Captions such as "Late 1890's Ball Gown" and "Late 1890's Fancy Promenade Suit" describe the designs in her catalog, along with corsets, corset covers and other "unmentionables" intended to be worn under those designs.

F⊕LKWEAR™

JAPANESE HAPI AND HAORI

FOLKWEAR ETHNIC PATTERNS, Box 3798, San Rafael, California 94912. Folkwear was begun by two California women in response to a growing interest in ethnic clothing. Their line of traditional folkwear patterns and fine antique clothing includes such exotic descriptions as an Afghani Nomad Dress, a Turkish Coat, Japanese Field Clothing, a Black Forest Smock, and a Nepali Blouse. There is a special group of Early American designs including a Prairie Dress and Missouri River Boatman's Shirt.

A brief sketch of the history of each design is included in the pattern envelope. Design authenticity is so respected that museum shops across the country are selling Folkwear Patterns.

Patterns are complete with instructions for whatever needlecraft is indigenous to the area of origin, be it embroidery, applique, quilting, smocking, or crochet. A range of sizes is complete in each pattern and there are designs for adults and children.

PAULOA PATTERNS, P.O. Box 11254, Honolulu, Hawaii 96828. Pauloa is a source for authentic Hawaiian, Polynesian, and Oriental patterns. Their mail-order catalog contains more than 100 styles of contemporary and classic styles, plus Hawaiian quilting and needlepoint patterns. Sarongs, holoku (an island bridal gown), muumuus, aloha shirts, and a Japanese Hapi coat, plus swimsuits and resort wear, are a few of the designs sketched in their brochure. Patterns are sized for both children and adults.

AUTHENTIC PATTERNS, P.O. Box 4560 Stockyard Station, Ft. Worth, Texas 76106. This company began with an extensive selection of square dance patterns and grew to include a full range of classic Western wear, including riding jackets and pants, hunt coats and jodhpurs, chaps to make of leather, Western shirts, and ponchos. Patterns are for both children and adults.

PARSON TABLE POINTERS

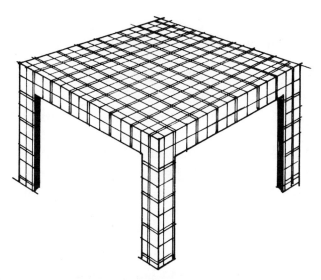

Remember a few years ago when plastic Parson's tables were such a hot item? Even drug stores sold them...for snack tables, for the patio, to hold plants. But after a few months' exposure to everyday use and weather, the finish was scratched, dull, and discolored.

If you have a couple of those tables still collecting dust, you may wish to cover them with fabric to lend an elegant designer touch to a bedroom, living room, or family room.

I completed this project in a mere hour and ten minutes, beginning with a search for the glue and yardstick and ending as I glued the last edge in place. No sewing is required; the hard part was finding the glue.

FABRIC
At a close-out sale of designer decorator fabric, I found a 100% cotton remnant, with a marblized pattern in shades of natural and brown.

Inexpensive as it was, the fabric was perfect for several reasons. The overall pattern required no pattern matching. Weight was sufficient so folds would be unobstrusive. The medium to dark color made fabric opaque. Fabric was tightly woven so stretching would be minimal.

CUTTING

Estimate fabric needs by measuring table and making a diagram. My 16-inch table, for example, was measured as follows: Each leg measures 16 inches from floor to table top and 9 inches around. Add one inch to each dimension: 17 x 10 inches.

The top measures 21 inches from base of apron to opposite side. Add two inches to each dimension: 23 x 23 inches. (See diagram.) Draw cutting lines directly on fabric, using a yardstick and soap or fabric marker.

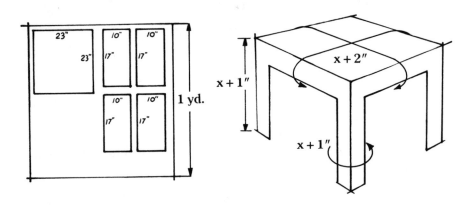

GLUING

Place table upside down and cover one leg at a time. Seams should be on the inside of the legs. Apply a thin strip of Elmer's glue along one long edge of each piece of fabric cut for legs.

Fold one-half inch to wrong side along glued edge.

Apply a thin strip of glue on wrong side of remaining long edges. Press fabric in place and wrap snugly around table legs. Make a cut at the apron to allow fabric to wrap smoothly.

Apply a final strip of glue along length of table leg to secure the folded fabric edge. Fabric should overlap table top by about one-half inch. Glue overlap in place. Glue and tuck in excess fabric at base of leg.

Once legs are completed, turn table upright. Dot glue on table top and center fabric on table. Fold fabric corners diagonally so they'll appear to be mitered. Dot a bit of glue under each corner and smooth in place.

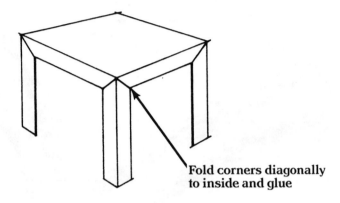

Fold corners diagonally to inside and glue

Invert table and apply a thin strip of glue along fabric edges. Smooth fabric to underside of the apron.

A clear glass top cut to size costs only a few dollars, will give your table a finished look, and protect the fabric as well.

This is one project you really must try—you'll love the results!

PILLOW TALK

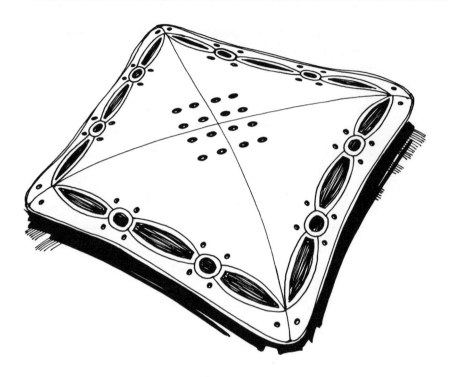

Brightly colored throw pillows are a terrific way to add color and style to a room, your decorator advises. How about a dozen little pillows to add excitement to your conversation pit? Let's see, at $20 each, those custom-made pillows will cost well over (gasp!) $200.

Tell your decorator you don't sew all that well, but you're a whiz at pillows. Now for a brief pillow-making lesson:

•Pillow covers should fit snugly. To measure, wrap a tape measure around the entire pillow; divide that measurement in half to obtain the dimensions of one side.

•Eliminating piping on a pillow may be a time saver, but it doesn't make for a good-looking pillow (except on a Turkish pillow). So don't skip the piping.

Use the piping typically sold with sewing notions. However, if the color you need is unavailable, check in the drapery and slip-cover notions area.

Pre-covered piping is inexpensive and much more fun than covering cording yourself. In fact, before selecting a fabric, I always check first to see that matching or coordinating piping is available. No sense in turning a small, fun project into drudgery!

This mitered pillow design can be adapted to any size square pillow. Choose a medium-weight striped fabric, wide wale corduroy, or a small scale border print.

PATTERN

For a theoretical 14-inch square pillow, draw a 14-inch square on newspaper. Connect corners with an X to make four triangles. On one triangle add a ¹/₄ inch seam allowance to each side. Cut out this triangle to use as a pattern.

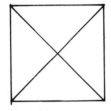 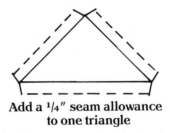

Add a ¹/₄″ seam allowance
to one triangle

One side of a pillow cover consists of four triangles. The mitered design may be used on both front and back or if you're short on fabric, cut the pillow back from plain fabric.

CUTTING

For one side, cut four <u>identical</u> triangles. Identical is the key word in cutting triangles which will create a mitered design. Select a stripe or point on fabric on which to place the base of each triangle in laying out pattern for cutting.

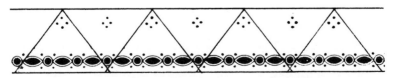

Cut 4 identical triangles to produce a mitered pattern

SEWING

•Seam together two pairs of triangles. Since these are bias seams, it will be easy to stretch and ease the stripes to match. Quarter-inch seam allowances are used throughout.

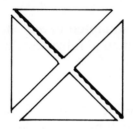

First seam two pairs of triangles together

Then seam together the 2 pairs

•Seam together the two large triangles to form a square. Repeat for pillow back (or simply cut a square).

•Stitch piping to right side of pillow cover front. Piping does not work well on square corners. So before stitching, draw a stitching guide to uniformly round corners. If you don't have a curved ruler, grab a coffee cup.

•Place two squares right sides together, piped side on top. Pin randomly, using only six or seven pins to keep fabric layers from sliding. Since squares are the same size, align edges and stitch just inside the previous row of stitching which secured piping.

Stitch around three sides of the pillow, leaving an opening centered on the fourth side through which to insert the pillow form.

•Close opening with invisible hand stitching after inserting pillow.

SUMMER

Summer sewing is especially fun because it's the closest thing to immediate gratification. How long can it take to make a strapless camisole or a bathing suit? In addition, casual, warm weather clothing is often unstructured and doesn't require a great deal of fitting.

You'll find many nearly instantly gratifying projects in this section, including camisoles, swimsuits, an apron, placemats and napkins, and a turkish pillow.

Under the heading "Speedy Sweatbands" you'll find instructions for making both a headband and wristband for tennis or running, plus how-to's for dressing up a towel.

Do you ever feel it's a waste of time to make something so inexpensive as a wristband or headband? I imagine I would if I didn't make them from scraps that would be otherwise thrown away.

There was one time this project was a real help. My children's elementary school has a Christmas boutique each year. Mothers make things by the dozens to help stock the boutique shelves. I was asked to make two dozen of anything and have the items ready by a certain date.

I work well under pressure, which is fortunate because I'm always under the pressure of some deadline or other. The night before I was to send my two dozen of "anything" to school with my children, I cut out 12 headbands and 12 wristbands and stitched them up before midnight.

The apron found in "Apron Applications" is a fun project. In summer this apron makes a good hostess gift, particularly if you're invited to a cookout.

The placemats and napkins found in "Pretty Placemats and Nifty Napkins" are easy sewing. Cooking isn't one of my favorite pastimes. I'm all for eating out as often as possible. Anywhere—fast food is fine. Just so I don't have to cook and clean up.

When I cook, I like to think if I use pretty cloth napkins, no one will notice we're having soup and sandwiches again.

The section entitled "Sheet Magic" may surprise you. It surprised me to discover that a $16 king size sheet equals six yards of 54-inch wide fabric priced at $3 per yard.

Linen manufacturers do a wonderful job in designing beautiful sheets. I hope you have fun reading about projects for utilizing those wonderful fabrics.

CREATE A CAMISOLE

One of summer's most versatile, wearable designs is the camisole top. Made up in terry or cotton knit, a camisole is ideal to wear with jeans and shorts. In a silk-like fabric, it's the perfect companion for a suit or linen blazer.

With the pattern below and a mere half yard of 45-inch fabric, you can sew up a camisole in less time than you could shop for one. The pattern is basic and you'll have fun adding your own variations for a creative, personal touch.

CUTTING
Make a pattern or mark cutting lines directly on fabric. On a folded length of fabric, draw a rectangle 20 inches wide, 15 inches deep on the fold, and tapering to 13 inches on the cut edge.

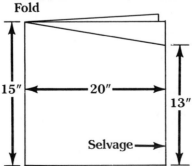

The finished camisole front will measure 13 inches deep; the back will measure 11 inches. Fit will be determined by the elastic length used to gather up the top and bottom. There is a single center back seam.

Again, this is a very basic pattern which may be graded down to fit a child or enlarged to fit a larger adult. Just keep these guidelines in mind: For length, allow one inch for each casing and two or more inches for "blousing". For width, add six to ten inches to body measurement.

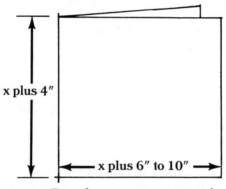

x plus 4"

◄— x plus 6" to 10" —►

**To make your own custom size
pattern x equals body measurement.**

SEWING

Bypass, for now, trimming, tucks, and other details in order to understand the basic sewing how-to:

•Stitch center back seam and press open. Using a sewing gauge, turn under one inch along both upper and lower edges. No need to baste—simply pin these one-inch turn-ups in place.

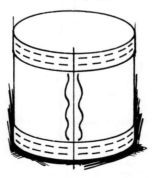

On both upper and lower edges, turn up one inch, stitch close to cut edge; stitch again $5/8"$ from first row of stitching.

•On wrong side, stitch close to raw edge of hem. Stitch a second time ⅝ inch from the first row of stitching. Complete these two rows of stitching on both upper and lower casings.

NOTE
The above instructions are given with a knit fabric in mind. If a woven is used, edges must be finished in some manner—perhaps with a three-step zigzag or an overcasting stitch. If your machine is not equipped to finish a raw edge, allow an extra inch when cutting and turn under each edge half an inch before making casings.

•Cut two strips of ½-inch elastic: one strip should be 2 inches smaller than waist measurement; the other strip should be 2 inches smaller than the upper bust measurement. On the wrong side, make a tiny clip into each casing. Pull elastic through. Before securing elastic ends, try on camisole to check for fit.

ANOTHER NOTE
You may be thinking how much quicker it would be to stitch elastic directly to camisole in lieu of making a casing and pulling through elastic. You'll find, however, elastic won't stretch as far as needed and casings are necessary after all.

VARIATIONS
Now for the fun part. With the above technique in mind, you may be as creative as you wish:

•Make an old-fashioned camisole of white dotted swiss, adding rows of lace and ribbons. For shoulder straps, pull ribbon through eyelet edging.

•Create design interest by dissecting pattern into bold color segments. Remember, gathers will visually narrow stripes. Try, for example, stitching together three 7-inch wide strips of cotton knit, perhaps of green, yellow, and red. Cut the back without a center seam, and add side seams.

•Use terry and dissect pattern crosswise. Combine, for instance, a 5-inch wide red strip with a 10-inch wide navy strip and sandwich white piping between the two.

•Encircle the upper edge of a camisole with a gathered ruffle of extra wide eyelet trim.

•Add bands of color by stitching rows of ribbon or single fold bias tape down camisole front.

•Sew a row of buttons down the center front.

•Experiment with tucks on this simple camisole before tackling a more complicated tucked dress or blouse pattern.

STITCH A SWIMSUIT

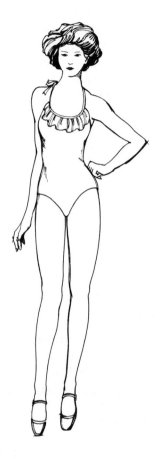

1:30 p.m. Begin with a swimsuit pattern and only ⁵/₈ yard of swimwear fabric—you may spend as much for the pattern as you do for fabric (Yes dear, the same fabric found in suits selling from $40 to $50 in ready-to-wear).

2:00 p.m. Suit is cut out and ready to sew.

2:30 p.m. Sewing is completed down to elastic in legs and straps—time to try on suit to check for fit.

3:00 p.m. Ready to swim!

Honestly! It's that easy to make a swimsuit. If you enjoy sunning or swimming, and if you make only one garment this summer, it must be a swimsuit.

Its size alone means a swimsuit is quick to sew, and there's really nothing magic in the sewing techniques. The miracle fibers used in swimwear today are strong, yet have enough stretch to make obsolete the armor-like underpinnings used a few years ago.

FABRIC
Fabric specifically intended for swimsuits is knitted with two-way stretch. While you may find swimwear fabric in the $10 to $20 range, look a little further to find $5 to $8 a yard fabric for your first venture.

PATTERNS
Simplicity, Vogue, McCall's, and Butterick all offer swimsuit patterns as does Stretch and Sew. While each may offer attractive designs, I've found Stretch and Sew does the best job on sewing techniques which produce professional results.

Stretch and Sew patterns, for example, are cut with a quarter inch seam allowance. Other commercial patterns give a $5/8$ inch seam allowance and then instruct the seam to be trimmed to a quarter inch. Perhaps it is felt this "just-in-case" extra seam allowance is needed; I feel it wastes fabric and time.

Stretch and Sew instructs elastic to be sewn directly to the fabric just as is done in fine ready-made swimwear. Other pattern makers instruct that a casing be stitched and elastic pulled through, for a "made-with-loving hands-at-home" look.

HOW-TO'S
With just a bit of background information, you'll be absolutely delighted at how simple it is to sew a swimsuit:

•Two-way stretch swimwear fabric has the greatest amount of stretch running lengthwise on the bolt, contrary to most knits which have stretch running across the bolt. The greatest amount of stretch goes around the body, so pattern pieces are laid crosswise, not up and down along selvage. Before cutting, consult pattern layout guide to be sure you understand this special layout consideration.

•Use a size 9 or 11 (65 or 75) ballpoint needle. Dispose of needle once swimsuit is completed as the Lycra and elastic dull the needle. Stretch each seam as it is sewn to put "give" into seams. Stitch stress seams twice, the second row of stitching $1/8$ inch from the first. If a $5/8$ inch seam allowance is used, trim seam allowance close to second row of stitching. Or if you're fortunate enough to have a machine which seams and overcasts in one step, use one of the stretch stitches for a light, stretchy fabric.

•Close seams and join ends of elastic. Stitch elastic to garment rather than using a casing: Divide swimsuit and elastic into quarters, marking quarter points with straight pins. Place elastic on wrong side of fabric close to edge. Stretch elastic to fit suit as you stitch, using a medium width length zigzag stitch. Turn elastic to inside and zigzag a second time, stretching elastic and suit as before.

Place elastic close to edge and zigzag.

Turn elastic and zigzag again.

GO ANYWHERE CANVAS TOTE

Can anyone possibly do without a washable canvas bag—to carry suntan oil, magazines, and camera to the beach; to tote wet bathing suits home from the pool; to carry those small bags home from the fruit market.

The following pattern is basically a rectangle folded in half, sides stitched, and handles sewn in place. What you do to the rectangle before it's folded and stitched will give the bag your own brand of style and touch of individuality:

•Fasten handles to upper edge of a navy poplin bag and add brightly colored pockets of varying sizes for sunglasses, keys, and change.

•If you're an artist, paint fruits and vegetables, using acrylic paints, to make a bag for marketing.

•Applique´ boating or golfing motifs...or whatever depicts your interests.

•Use purchased webbing for handles.

•Select an unusual decorator fabric instead of the typical canvas or denim.

•Shop for unusual hardware: metal studs, D-rings, zippers or buckles.

CUTTING

The finished dimensions of the basic bag are $14^{1}/_{2}$ by $15^{1}/_{2}$ inches, cut from one yard of 60-inch denim. Cut two rectangles 30 by 16 inches, one for bag and one for lining. Cut on the selvage edges two handles each $3^{1}/_{2}$ by 36 inches. Cut one bottom panel 16 by 16 inches. Cut two pockets, each 6 by 8 inches.

Clip notches to mark centers of bag, lining, and bottom panel Use $^{1}/_{4}$ inch seam allowances throughout.

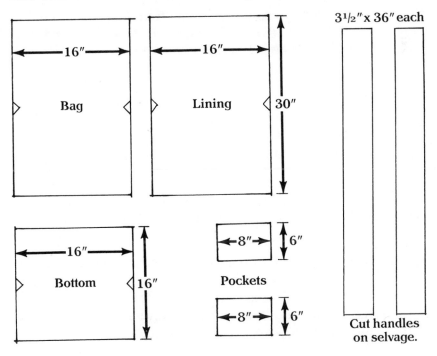

SEWING

•Press under ½ inch on upper edge of pockets and finish with two rows of topstitching, the first row close to edge, the second row about ⅜ inch from first row of topstitching.

•Press under ¼ inch on long edges of bottom panel. Align center notches of bottom panel and bag and temporarily pin panel in place.

•Center and pin pockets on either side of panel. The unfirnished sides of pockets will be covered by the handles; the lower edge of pockets will be covered by the bottom panel.

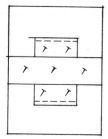

Handle

Press under ¼ inch, then cover with selvage and topstitch.

•To make handles, press under ¼ inch on long edge. Fold in half so selvage edge covers raw edge. Finish with two rows of topstitching along both long edges.

•Fold bottom panel toward center, away from pockets. Position handles to overlap pockets ½ inch. Stitch handles to bag, stopping two inches short of upper edges of bag.

•Smooth bottom panel over lower edges of pockets. Secure panel with two rows of topstitching along edges next to pockets.

•Fold bag in half, right sides together, and stitch side seams. Repeat for lining. Press under ½ inch along upper edge of bag and lining.

•Insert lining in bag, wrong sides together. Match side seams and pin folded edges together. Stitch around bag opening, sewing through bag and lining. Bag may be left flat or corners may be squared by turning bag inside out and sewing diagonally across side seams at base.

SPEEDY SWEATBANDS

Tennis anyone? How about jogging or playing basketball or soccer in the hot sun?

All summertime action sports call for sweatbands, and once you've sewn a wristband and headband, you'll wish you were in business. Add a jazzed-up towel and you'll have a Father's Day gift set.

Begin with a good quality stretch terry with a high percentage of cotton fiber. Perhaps you'll have scraps to make a sweatband. If not, use the diagram to figure needed yardage, based on the number of bands you wish to make.

I happened to have a 1 1/2 yard remnant on hand and using a bit of basic math determined that 14 headbands and 14 wristbands could be made from this $3 cut of fabric. Going a step further, I figured if wristbands retail for $1 each and headbands sell for $2 each, a $3 investment multiplies out to $42. This causes me to ponder why I'm a writer and not a manufacturer, but makes me feel fortunate I have the option of sewing.

Back to the subject at hand: Should you have stretch terry scraps, both a wristband and a headband can be made in about 15 minutes, using the following steps:

Since stretch terry will be used, the dimensions given will fit a wide range of adult sizes. However, for the extremes—a small child or hulk-size adult—adjust the width 1/2 to 1 inch. Keep in mind, though, a soggy headband may droop over the eyes during a crucial moment with disasterous consequences for the seamstress responsible.

HEADBAND
•Cut a rectangle 22 by 6 inches, with the stretch being on the long edge.

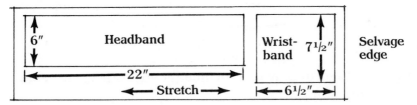

•Fold rectangle in half, matching short ends and right sides together. Machine stitch, using a quarter-inch seam allowance.
Smooth seam open.

•Fold headband in half, with one edge slightly overlapping the
other. Fold in half again so that headband is four layers thick.

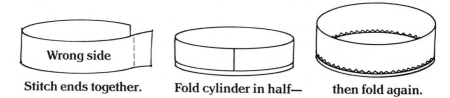

Stitch ends together.   Fold cylinder in half—   then fold again.

•With machine set on a long, narrow zigzag stitch, machine-
stitch along the raw edge.

This method sounds just too simple, but it works for two reasons: 1) stretch knit terry will not fray and the cut edge tends to
roll under; and 2) the zigzag stitches disappear into the plush
terry loops. Result: no raw edge and stitches won't show.

WRISTBAND
•Cut a rectangle 6 1/2 by 7 1/2 inches, with the stretch being on
the edge measuring 6 1/2 inches.

•Fold rectangle in half, matching ends measuring 7 1/2 inches,
right sides together. Machine stitch using a 1/4-inch seam allowance. Smooth seam open.

•Fold wristband in thirds, right sides out so that wristband is
three layers thick.

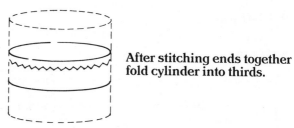

After stitching ends together
fold cylinder into thirds.

•Finish as described above for headband—zigzagging along
the cut edge.

SWEAT TOWEL

Purchase a hand towel and give it a customized look with one of the following:

•Stitch a border of red,white, and blue ribbon along each end. Be sure to stitch in the same direction on each side of ribbon to prevent rippling.

•If you are a tennis player, purchase a border trim with a tennis motif to stitch along towel ends.

•Add color to a towel by stitching several bands of bias tape to towel end.

•Spell out a name or appropriate title with iron-on calico letters. Don't trust fusible letters to adhere to the plush terry—reinforce by zigzagging around edges.

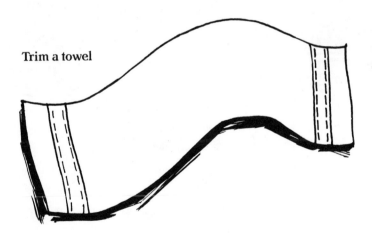

Trim a towel

UMBRELLA TABLE TREATS

A round umbrella table calls for a special tablecloth: one that will attractively cover the table without the fuss of having to first remove the umbrella. The solution, of course, is a wrap-around tablecloth.

To insure that this simple project remains simple, purchase a flannel-backed plastic circular tablecloth. Convert it to a wrap-around tablecloth by simply cutting a slit to the center of the cloth. Next, cut a small hole for the umbrella pole, and then finish the slit edges and hole.

The instructions which follow can be used to convert a plastic or fabric tablecloth; or should you have no luck in finding a ready-made cloth, you might wish to cut a circular cloth from a flat sheet.

Using the step-by-step instructions below, try to top my time of approximately fifty minutes:

•Fold a purchased round tablecloth in half, then in half again.

•Measure the diameter of the umbrella pole and add half an inch.

•On the folded cloth draw the quarter hole for the umbrella pole. A large spool or coin might be used as an aid for rounding the line.

•Draw a straight line from the cloth edge to the hole. This cut should be made on the straight of grain on a woven cloth. A plastic cloth, of course, has no grain, but checks or stripes might furnish a convenient straight cutting edge.

•After marking and checking cutting lines, cut from edge to center and remove the circle for the umbrella pole.

•Finish slit edges with two-inch wide bias hem facing. Cut two lengths of the facing, each one-half inch longer than the slit edge.

•One edge of the slit must overlap the other edge. For the upper lap, turn under about one-fourth inch along the cut edge. Fold the facing strip in half and place the double edges on the wrong side atop the folded over edge. Secure with zigzag stitches (See diagram.) A zigzag is preferable to a straight stitch because it requires less accuracy. Complete this step without pinning: fold a bit and stitch, then fold a bit more.

Wrong side

Fold ¼ inch to wrong side; cover with doubled bias hem facing

UPPERLAP

•For the underlap, fold the facing in half. Place the double edge of the facing on the right side of the cloth edge so that facing overlaps cloth about one-quarter inch. Zigzag close to facing edge. (See diagram.) Here again, no pinning is required: just smooth in place, sew a bit, then smooth a bit more.

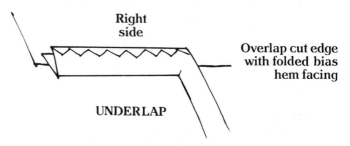

•The underlap facing lies flat, while the overlap facing folds under to the wrong side. Place the cloth on the table and mark two positions for Velcro fasteners: one close to the center hole and the other on the table top, near the table edge. Secure Velcro fasteners with zigzag stitching.

•Finish the hole and hem edge of the facings with an overcasting stitch or a medium length and width zigzag.

APRON APPLICATIONS

Do early-arriving dinner guests ever catch you darting about the kitchen in an old bathrobe because you just can't do last-minute chores in your party best? Enter the cover-all apron—an ideal project for the beginning seamstress because there is little to go wrong.

On the other hand, for the experienced, creative seamstress, the cover-all apron offers an opportunity to experiment with quilted pockets, appliqueś, fabric painting, and other customized sewing techniques.

What's more, you'll get two aprons for the price of one because the yardage for one or two aprons is the same: three-fourths yard of 45-inch fabric. In addition to fabric, each apron calls for $3^3/4$ yards of extra-wide, double-fold bias tape. Sew one for yourself and make an extra apron for a hostess gift in as little as an hour or two.

I made my two prototype aprons (costing about $6 for the two) in red quilted cotton bound in navy calico. However, canvas, poplin, denim, or any medium-weight fabric will produce great results for this project.

To get your creative wheels turning, here are some possible combinations:

•Trim navy and white ticking with red calico bias tape.

•Use crayon-bright colors to bind a denim apron—green across the top, yellow around the sides and neck, and red around the lower edge.

•Applique´a name or use iron-on letters to spell out an appropriate title.

•Add a quilted pocket to yellow terry, bound with parrot green.

•Experiment with double-needle quilting on pockets or the entire apron.

•Cooking isn't your thing? Customize your apron design for another activity such as gardening, lab work, sewing or painting with strategically shaped and positioned pockets.

•Applique´vegetables, golf clubs, butterflies, or whatever applique´will make the apron just right for the recipient.

•Make this a first sewing project for a youngster.

PATTERN
Trace pattern in back of book on folded tracing material. Open pattern and pin to a single thickness of fabric for quilteds, or cut two aprons from two layers of flat fabric.

BIAS TAPE BINDING
Note that one side of double- fold bias tape is slightly wider than the other. The wider side goes on the wrong side of the fabric. Stitching is done on right side.

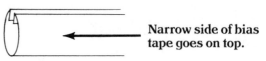

Working on right side slide fabric into bias tape, then topstitch close to edge.

Narrow side of bias tape goes on top.

Slide fabric edge into tape so that fabric edge butts the tape fold. Don't bother to pin. Simply position tape in a small area, stitch, stop to position tape, stitch again, and so on.

If you've ever worked with bias tape, you've probably discovered the weight of the presser foot tends to stretch the bias tape, causing puckering and rippling. This may be alleviated by using a zipper foot lowered to rest on the garment rather than on the tape.

APRON HOW-TO
Armed with pattern and the how-to for conquering bias tape rippling, you'll zip right through:

•Finish upper raw edge of apron with machine overcasting or simply turn under raw edge and straight stitch. Turn a 3/4 inch hem to inside and pin in place.

•Apply bias tape to lower edge of apron.

Apply bias tape to lower edge. ⟶

•Cut an 82-inch length of bias tape for binding the remaining edges, to create neck loop, and to furnish ties. Extra inches might be needed for a tall cook, so estimate with a tape measure.

Anchor bias tape to apron so that a 19-inch tie extends. Beginning at tie end, machine stitch through tape. With tape encasing curved side edge, continue stitching. Stitch around neck loop, along remaining side, and to end of tie. (See diagram.) Knot tie ends or finish with a close zigzag stitch.

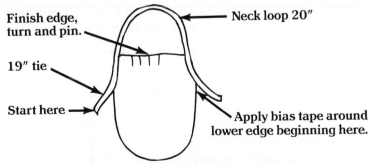

Finish edge, turn and pin.

Neck loop 20″

19″ tie

Start here ⟶

Apply bias tape around lower edge beginning here.

•Embellish apron with pockets, appliqués, or iron-ons.

PRETTY PLACEMATS AND NIFTY NAPKINS

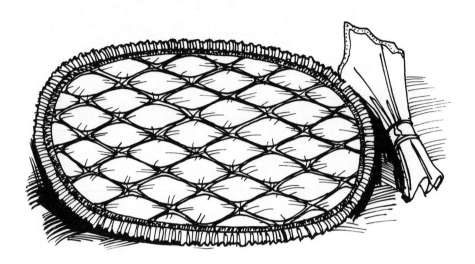

Home sewing statistics indicate that sewing related to crafts and decorating comprises nearly half of all sewing done by American women. Perhaps it's because in these areas we can enjoy the creative aspects of sewing without the hassles of fitting.

Placemats and napkins are two of my favorite craft projects for the home. I'm always amazed when I compare the price of ready-made placemats and napkins with the cost of the fabric I use when I make them myself.

Six napkins, for example, can be made from 7/8 yard of 45-inch fabric. Six placemats require only one yard of 45-inch double-face quilted fabric, and 8 1/2 yards of bias trim.

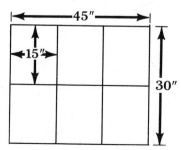

The selection of double-face quilteds with coordinating flat fabrics has never been greater. Single-face quilteds are widely available too, and turn out very nicely bound with double-fold bias tape.

PATTERNS

Though you'll probably find commercial patterns available, a placemat on hand can simply be traced. Or you may wish to experiment with various shapes—a trapazoid for use on a round table, for instance. Keep in mind, however, that square corners must be mitered and that sewing will be simplified if corners are rounded.

HOW-TO

Trace placemat shape on quilted fabric (an oval placemat pattern is included in the back of this book), and cut placemats of single thickness.

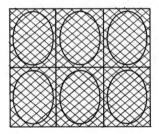

Before binding, consider the following guidelines:

•Binding will be partially sewn to the placemat and the ends joined, before completely stitching the binding to placemat.

•To guard against miscalculations and to reduce waste, allow binding to feed from the uncut length, rather than cutting a length for each platemat.

•Straight stitching will be a breeze as the standard sewing machine foot, when aligned with fabric edge, sews $1/4$ inch from the fabric edge—the ideal width for the binding.

•Finished binding should be smooth and uniform in width. And it will be if, when initially stitched to placemat, the binding is unstretched and sewn exactly $1/4$ inch from the edge.

To apply binding:

•Determine the "right" side of the double-face quilted. Begin on a straight edge of the placemat with binding on right side of quilted, placing right sides together. Leaving a 3-inch "tail", stitch binding to placemat. Stitch around placemat, stopping 4 inches short of where stitching began. Back-stitch to lock stitching and remove work from machine.

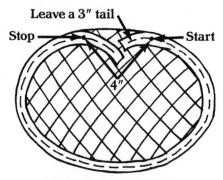

•Cut binding so that ends overlap about 1½ inches. Place ends at right angles, right sides together, and machine stitch from corner to corner. Pin before stitching and check to see that binding strip is the correct length.

•Stitch remaining 4 inches of binding strip to placemat. This sounds a great deal more complicated than it actually is. You may be inclined to simply place ends together and stitch, but the above method produces a much more professional look and is really no more difficult.

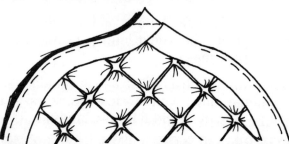

•Press binding away from placemat. With a box of pins and sewing gauge in hand, find a comfortable chair for this next step. Smooth binding to wrong side of placemat. Fold under raw edge of binding and pin, keeping pins perpendicular to the seam line for easy removal during sewing.

•Working on right side of placemat, topstitch close to seam line. Because the pressure of the presser foot tends to stretch the binding, causing a rippling effect, I use a zipper foot set to rest on the left side of the needle. The weight of the foot then rests on the placemat rather than the binding, resulting in little or no rippling.

NAPKINS

Napkins are speedily made—only three minutes to completely machine finish the edges. The secret is in a nifty "overcasting foot" available through your Viking Sewing Machine dealer. This foot, costs only a few dollars and is available in three sizes. The overcasting foot turns an ordinary zigzag stitch into an overcasting stitch, giving a finish similar to that found on ready-made napkins. To be sure you purchase the proper size foot, take along your machine's standard foot when you shop.

Whether or not you plan to make napkins, you'll be able to overcast facing, hem, and seam edges on other projects. No explanation for using this foot is really necessary—just a few tips:

•After attaching foot to machine, set machine on widest zigzag. The length of the zigzag, which will control the closeness of the stitches, will vary with personal preference and fabric weight. My Viking, for example, with a length gauge from zero to six, works best set between zero and one. Before stitching, manually operate machine to be sure needle doesn't strike foot.

•Fabric edge should rest against the guide which protrudes from the underside of the foot.

•When overcasting napkins, or anything with right angles, I find it easier to sew one complete side, lock stitches, and remove work from machine. Then sew another side as a unit, rather then pivoting at corners. Even including starting and stopping time, you'll amaze yourself by turning out napkins at the rate of one every three minutes.

PRESENTING PANEL PRINTS

Have you ever purchased a piece of fabric just because it was beautiful or interesting? An exquisite print, perhaps, which could never be made into a garment, yet was too bold for draperies or slipcovers?

Some of my favorite fabrics are groups of panel prints by Cyrus Clark of England. These prints are silk-screened on cotton chintz and sold by the panel in groups of three. Each panel consists of three 11½" by 13½" related prints such as seashells, wild flowers and butterflies, costing only a few dollars.

While these Cyrus Clark panel prints are certainly reasonably priced, many graphic textiles are priced at a real premium, costing as much as $30-$40 per yard. If you enjoy beautifully printed fabric, watch for it in unexpected places at more affordable prices.

Towels, sheets, pillow cases, table cloths, and linen dish towels, for example, may offer interesting designs. Decorator and upholstery fabrics are another source of printed fabric, generally costing less than graphic textiles.

Photograph Courtesy of Cincinnati Enquirer

What to do with a beautiful fabric find? A bold print used sparingly may be striking, while too many yards of a bold print may be overwhelming. Here are some interesting ways to use prints in small quantities of striking fabric:

•Cover a corkboard with fabric for a unique buttetin board to hang by the phone or in a child's room.

•Cover a chair seat. If the panel is too small, enlarge it with fabric strips. Avoid a close-but-not-quite match by choosing an obvious contrast.

For example, it's unlikely that the dark brown chintz background of my seashell print could be matched with an identical solid. A cream velveteen, however, might offer a more interesting contrast and is easily found.

To enlarge a panel, first sew strips to sides, then add longer strips to encompass strips and panel.

To enlarge a panel with fabric strips, cut and sew strips the length of the panel to two sides. Then cut and sew strips long enough to encompass both the panel and the two strips.

•Make a wall hanging. Stretcher bars especially for stretching fabric panels are available but may be expensive for very large panels.

Consider less costly alternatives to serve as stretchers: styrofoam panels packed around small appliances might furnish a frame to wrap fabric around.

Or ask your favorite carpenter to tack together lumber scraps to make a frame. Purchase a 12 x 36 x 1 inch styrofoam panel at a hobby shop to cut in pieces for small panels. Shop for inexpensive picture frames. I found frames precisely the size I needed for $1 each. After wrapping fabric around frames, it was secured with a heavy-duty stapler.

•Make a pillow cover. To make my pillow cover more interesting, I trapuntoed a focal point. (For how-to's, see Timely Trapunto Tips.) Place a panel on each side of the pillow or use a panel on just one side and a solid color on the reverse side.

SHEET MAGIC

Have you ever wished for extra-wide fabric—the kind mills manufacture especially for linens and bedding?

Your wish will come true if you choose sheets the next time you're in need of such fabric. For example, a king-size sheet approximately 108 by 102 inches is equivalent to nearly six yards of 54-inch fabric. Therefore, a $16 king-size sheet costs out to less than $3 a yard for 54-inch wide fabric.

Perhaps you've thought of all the obvious things to make from sheets: tablecloths, draperies, and window coverings. But don't forget placemats, napkins, lamp shades, pillows, and window shades. Or a pretty flounced peasant dress from an eyelet ruffled sheet. Or the spectacular effect of covering walls with shirred sheeting.

COVER A WALL WITH SHIRRED SHEETING

Though peeling paint, buckling plaster, and pipes may be lurking beneath, covering a wall with shirred fabric is a most elegant wall treatment. It is also an affordable treatment when sheets are used.

Since shirring will hide sheet edges, the only sewing involved is to make ceiling and floor casings. The casings allow sheets to be removed and reused when you move or change your decorating theme.

Measure the width of the wall to be covered and buy sheets equal to that width, doubled. For example, a 9-foot wide wall (108 inches) would require two king-size sheets, 108 inches wide each. If you find sheets equal to 2 1/2 to 3 times the wall width, use them untrimmed as shirring will simply be a bit fuller.

For length, add 7 inches to floor-to-ceiling measurement; that is, two 3-inch hems, plus 1 inch for take-up when rods are inserted in casings.

For casings, turn a 3-inch hem to wrong side, both bottom and top. Turn under raw edge one-half inch. Machine stitch along turned up edge, then again 1 1/2 inches from top for a one inch wide casing.

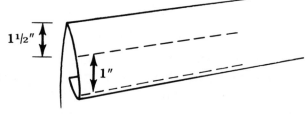

Note: Here it may be possible to utilize factory sheet hems. This possibility should be determined before cutting fabric to proper length.

Choose either of two methods of installation:

•Install cafe curtain brackets 1 1/2 inches from ceiling and 1 1/2 inches from floor. The number of brackets necessary will depend on the width of the wall and the weight of the shirred fabric. About every 2 feet should be sufficient. Hang rods on brackets and adjust gathers. To cover pipes or other protrusions, extension brackets may be used.

•A second method is to make casings only 3/4 inch wide instead of 1 inch wide. Pull a heavy cord through completed casings. Tie cord to nails at either end. After evenly distributing gathers, staple sheets at intervals for support.

GATHERED LAMP SHADE
Sheet-weight fabric is ideal for lampshades. In addition, leftover sheet fabric can be used to make coordinating pillows and a dust ruffle. The same technique used to make a lampshade can also be used to cover a waste basket or plant container.

To determine the amount of fabric to cut, measure the circumference of the widest end of the lamp shade. Double that figure. Measure the depth of the lampshade and add 4 inches. A shade measuring 48 inches around the bottom, and 14 inches in depth, for example, requires a length of fabric 96 by 18 inches.

Machine stitch together short ends of fabric to form a cylinder. Press under raw edges, then turn up a 5/8 inch wide casing on each edge.

Machine stitch casing in place. Stitch close to turned edge and leave an opening for inserting elastic. Pull 1/2 inch wide elastic through both casings, drawing up to ensure that the cover fits snugly.

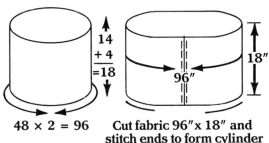

48 × 2 = 96   Cut fabric 96"x 18" and stitch ends to form cylinder

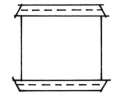

Turn under raw edges, then turn up 5/8" casings. Stitch casings in place, leaving opening to insert elastic

OVAL TABLECLOTH

Covering a large oval table will, at best, be expensive and at worst, impossible for a non-standard size table.

To make your own custom-sized oval cloth, start with a sheet of adequate size. Twin sheets measure 66 by 96 inches; double sheets 81 by 96; queen-size sheets 90 by 102; and king-size sheets 108 by 102.

Center the sheet on the table and anchor with heavy books so fabric won't shift during marking. Cloth should have an 8 to 12-inch drop plus a 1/2 inch hem allowance. Arrange fabric so that straight of grain is square on table. Use a ruler and fabric marker to mark base of drop from table top.

To finish the tablecloth edge, select one of the following options:

•Use a narrow hemmer attachment;

•Turn hem edge to right side and cover with purchased braid, fringe, or single fold bias tape; or

•Finish raw edge with a three-step zigzag stitch. Turn a 1/4 inch hem to wrong side and secure with a straight stitch machine hem.

TANTALIZING TURKISH PILLOWS

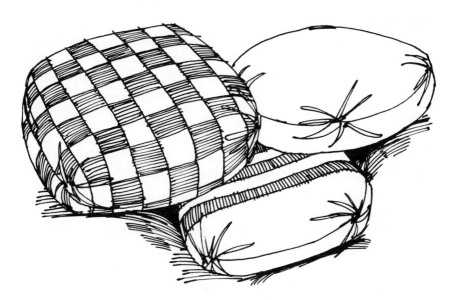

Browsing through an exclusive interior design studio, I saw a custom-made sofa casually strewn with six colorful, clever-looking Turkish pillows. Each pillow was a small square, covered with a soft cotton fabric, and sewn with the simplest of sewing techniques. Each pillow cost $19.

Knowing that one yard of fabric yields three small pillow covers, and mentally picturing my stack of shabby looking pillows at home, I could hardly wait to begin their transformation.

Even if you're less than a pro when it comes to sewing, your Turkish pillows are certain to be a success because cording is unnecessary and if the pillow form is at least fourteen inches, a closure is not needed.

Turkish pillows are quite versatile. Very large ones make great floor cushions, medium-size ones will transform a bed into a couch, and smaller pillows can be used as color accents on a bed or sofa.

The shape of a Turkish pillow might be square or oblong. A soft, loose pillow form is preferable to a solid, firm pillow form because a cushiony, plump look is desirable. Choose a soft, drapeable fabric as well.

MEASURING
Begin by measuring the pillow form to be covered. It's easier and more accurate to wrap a tape measure around the entire pillow and then to divide that measurement by two, rather than to measure across the pillow.

CUTTING
To ensure a snug fit, the pillow cover should be slightly smaller than the pillow. This will be accomplished when the corners are tied. Half-inch seam allowances are used throughout.

After measuring the pillow, draw two rectangles on fabric to match the dimensions of the pillow, plus one inch added to each dimension for seam allowances. A 17-inch square pillow, for example, calls for two 18-inch squares.

SEWING
Place the fabric covers right sides together and stitch around three sides. The fourth side, through which the pillow form will be inserted, requires a bit of explanation:

The pillow's gathered corners are formed by tying each corner into a "rabbit ear" with twine. This step takes about two inches from each corner.

The opening, therefore, must be centered and large enough to insert the pillow form, and still have two or three extra inches of fabric on either end for gathering and tying. A pillow smaller than about fourteen inches square will require a zipper centered on the pillow back for inserting the pillow form.

After closing three sides and the ends of the fourth side, press open seams. Before turning cover, use twine to tie each corner into a "rabbit ear" about two inches long in order to create the gathered corners.

Leave opening ——→

Tie each corner into a rabbit ear.

Turn cover and insert pillow form. Close opening with hand stitching.

FALL

When my daughter and son were very young, I would tuck them in bed and often sew till 2 or 3 a.m. I suppose it was simply to obtain some tangible evidence of accomplishment so much needed after a day of doing and re-doing the chores that are part of a young mother's life.

Amy and Scott are older now and I still find a great deal of satisfaction in sewing. Sewing enables me to be creative; to enjoy beautiful things; and to experience that sense of accomplishment each time I 'create'.

The Fall season is a wonderful time for 'creating', what with vacations over and children back to school. Making special school bags has become an annual ritual in our family. The school bag you'll read about in this section was the all-time favorite..

This particular bag is quick to sew, leaving time for machine applique or other special trim treatments.

Next time you make a vest, be sure to try the construction technique described in "Very Important Vest". Each time I use this method I feel as though I've performed magic.

If you enjoy employing ingenuity, you'll find projects in this season especially for you: "Recycling: Unclaimed Riches" and "Home Grown Sewing Aids."

My favorite Fall project is the Christmas tree. A pattern for the tree is on the master sheet found at the back of the book so you won't have to search for graph paper to enlarge a diagram.

I adore sewing projects such as the mohair and Ultrasuede® coat described in "Classy Coats." But I enjoy just as much (well, almost as much) sewing things for children.

Children are easy to fit and of course small garments can be sewn quickly. If you're learning to sew or returning to sewing, think of sewing children's wear as prerequisite work for more demanding projects. I hope the tips for sewing for children found in the last segment of this season help.

SCHOOL DAYS SCHOOL BAG

Making a school bag with machine-sewn appliqués is a good way to learn a new sewing skill and, at the same time, delight a child. Even if no one in your life currently needs a school bag, you might still enjoy learning about machine appliqué.

 Photograph Courtesy of Cincinnati Enquirer

FABRIC

Use denim or canvas for the school bag, along with a brightly-printed cotton or blend fabric for the lining. For two school bags, one yard of denim and 7/8 yard of lining are needed. The yardage requirement is the same for either one or two bags, so two bags can be made for the cost of one.

A variety of fabrics may be used for the applique. Corduroy, pique, suede cloth and quilteds lend surface texture; tiny prints with brightly colored grounds furnish color.

In planning an applique design, remember that rickrack, bias tape, buttons, and other trims can be incorporated for additional design interest. Green rickrack, for example, might be used for grass; or button flowers might grow on green bias tape stems.

APPLIQUE'

My favorite applique pattern is one by Vogue which has been around for years. Patterns change, but subjects ideal for applique seem destined to stay around—flowers, animals, sun/clouds, and other simple shapes. Numbers and an alphabet are also quite suitable.

Most pattern transfers are meant to be used only once and then discarded. A heat transfer pencil, however, can be used to trace a transfer to make it as good as new.

Machine applique isn't only for school bags of course. It's a terrific custom touch for all sorts of boutique items—from poplin wrap skirts and canvas Bermuda bags to suede handbags and Ultrasuede® belts. Use the following step-by-step instructions to create your own distinctive look:

• Pin a backing layer of Pellon's "Stitch-n-Tear" or a non-fusible lightweight interfacing to wrong side of fabric to which applique will be sewn.

• Fuse featherweight interfacing to the wrong side of the applique fabric. Apply heat transfer pattern to the right side of the interfaced fabric.

•Cut out applique pieces and arrange on school bag. Secure pieces temporarily with Glue Stick, a washable fabric adhesive.

•Permanently secure appliqués with a wide, close zigzag stitch after experimenting with your machine to determine the best stitch setting. In stitching, the needle should fall just off the edge of the applique so that stitches fall on the applique rather than on the background fabric.

•Add dimension to an applique by leaving a small opening and pushing in fiberfill with a pencil before completing the zigzag stitching.

SCHOOL BAG

For each school bag, cut from denim or canvas: one 16 by 28 inch rectangle; two handles cut on the selvage, each 3 by 16 inches; and one pocket 12 by 6 inches. From lining fabric, cut a 16 by 28 inch rectangle.

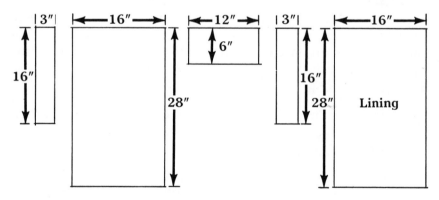

Denim or Canvas

Complete applique and pockets after cutting while fabric is still flat. Sew pocket as follows:

•Determine center of pocket and bag by folding each in half. Mark center folds with soap. Center pocket about 5 inches from the upper edge of the bag.

•Press under sides and bottom edges of the pocket. I encased the upper pocket edge with red bias tape to add a bit of color.

However, this edge could be finished in the same way as the sides and bottom. Either finish upper edge of pocket with bias tape or turn under and topstitch twice.

•Pin or Glue Stick pocket into place and secure with two rows of topstitching.

•Divide pocket into three segments with two rows of topstitching.

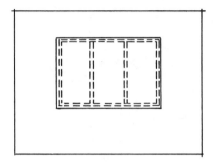

To complete bag:

•Fold bag in half, right sides together, and close side seams. Repeat for lining.

•Make handles by folding raw edge toward center. Fold over selvage edge so handles are folded in thirds. Topstitch twice on either side. Then stitch handles to bag.

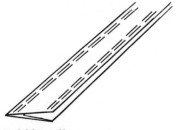

Fold handles in thirds and topstitch twice along each edge.

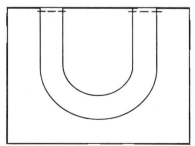

Attach handle to each side.

•Press open seams of both school bag and lining. Square off corners of bag and lining by stitching diagonally across each corner.

•Turn school bag right side out and slip inside lining so lining and bag are right sides together.

•Align side seams and pin lining to bag along upper edge of bag. Machine stitch along upper edge, leaving a four-inch opening for turning.

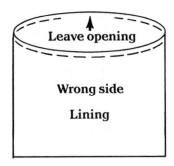

•Pull bag through lining; turn lining into bag. Smooth and pin edge so that seam rolls inside bag. Topstitch twice along upper edge to reinforce handles as well as to close the opening left for turning.

•Breathe a sigh of relief as you wave goodbye to the school bus.

RECYCLING: UNCLAIMED RICHES

Recycling is always a good idea, and there may be times in each of our lives when it may become a real necessity. Perhaps the ideas below will help you squeeze a bit more service from the things you wear and use:

CLOTHING IN GENERAL

•The obvious, of course, is to make a small garment from a large garment. This is worthwhile only when the large garment is of good quality fabric. That full bias-cut wool skirt that makes you appear twice as wide as you are, might be utilized to make a slim skirt, a vest, or a child's skirt.

•Save brightly-colored knit shirts for incorporating color as sleeves, pockets, collars, yokes, and trim when making new knit garments.

SUEDE AND LEATHER

•Narrow those five-inch outdated lapels on a still gorgeous suede blazer. It may be possible to simply restitch lapel edges using either one or two rows of top stitching, then trim close to stitching.

•Make a small cowboy a fringed vest from a suede jacket.

•Make an entire vest or just a vest front of suede.

•From suede or leather, cut elbow patches, a leather collar and cuffs, cover buttons, or make pockets. Use narrow strips of suede or leather to trim a collar. Cut a buttonband of suede for a jacket.

•Make a belt.

•Use leather for the yoke of a jacket.

SWEATERS

•Take that long-sleeve angora pullover—still like new, but matching nothing in your closet. Slit the pullover down the front, and bind edges with Ultrasuede. If you're low on Ultrasuede, make a dress and bind the sweater edges with dress fabric for a two-piece ensemble.

•Make a warm pull-on cap for winter.

•Cut off the sleeves of a seldom worn sweater and make a vest.

•A serious recycler will trim and save the ribbing from a stained or torn sweater and use it to trim a wool jacket or dress.

MAN'S SHIRT

The shirt looks fine except for the fraying cuffs and collar. The obvious solution (does anyone really take the time to do this?): remove the collar and cuffs and reverse them so that the worn side is inside.

Instead, it's much more fun if you find a man whose shirts fit you through the shoulders to remake the shirt to fit you. Cut off the collar, leaving only the collar stand. Sew narrow lace along the edge of the collar stand, then bind with bias tape. Apply the same treatment to the cuff edges of the shirt.

BATH TOWELS

•Your new biege-and-brown bathroom just isn't the place for your old pastel towels. Solution: dye them a dark color.

•Use towels as flat fabric from which to cut a bath or beach robe.

•Use towels to make a swim cover-up or lounging robe.

STAINED OR WORN TABLECLOTHS

•Use a stained tablecloth as a buffer under another tablecloth to prevent the table from shining through.

•Dye a stained tablecloth a dark color and frequently exclaim that brown is your favorite color.

SWEATER SOPHISTICATION

Designers say beautiful, distinctive sweaters are <u>THE</u> look this season: sweaters hand-knitted from heavy wool yarn; sweaters trimmed with delicate lace and satin ribbons; and sweaters lavishly embroidered.

Unfortunately, the price tags on many of these beauties may leave most of us out in the cold. Yet surprisingly, these up-to-the-minute sweaters may be much like the sweaters still around from years past.

Of course only magic can make a hand-knitted sweater from a mass-produced one, but ingenuity plus lace, ribbon, and other trims can work wonders. Need a few starter ideas?

•A white angora sweater, victim of a hungry moth, might be recycled with a sprinkling of bows concentrated around the front neckline. Use ¹/₈ inch wide pastel ribbon and a Dritz loop turner or crochet hook.

Working on the right side of the sweater, insert hook so that it comes back out on the right side ¹/₄ inch from the first insert.

Insert the hook between yarns to avoid damaging fibers. Hold a 3-inch length of ribbon in a loop. Catch loop with hook; and pull end through. Tie ribbon once and trim ends evenly.

This trim has to be the quickest, easiest, and least expensive update. Less than one yard of ribbon costing about 50¢ a yard is needed for a really great new look.

•Lend character to a cable knit sweater by running narrow ribbon through cables—again using a loop turner or crochet hook to pull ribbon through at equal intervals.

•Stitch 1/2 inch wide bands of satin ribbon to a sweater, running from shoulders and neckline downward, in graduated lengths. Tack a bow to the base of each band.

•For a designer look, add lace cutouts to a smooth knit, dressy sweater. This may be done with lace appliqués or strips of lace, using the same basic sewing technique for either:

For lace strips, mark placement lines on right side of the sweater. Pin and topstitch along lace edges, stopping 1/2 inch short of either end, again working on the right side.

On the wrong side, carefully slit sweater under lace, stopping 1/2 inch from ends. Cut remaining 1/2 inch into a wedge. Press seam allowances to either side away from lace insert. On right side, either zigzag or topstitch along the lace edge again to strengthen seam and to diminish fraying of the seam allowances should this method be used on a woven fabric.

For lace appliqués, use same technique as above. It may be impossible, however, to press the seam allowance away from an irregularly shaped lace appliqué. In this instance, trim seam allowance to about 1/4 inch then topstitch or zigzag a second time on the right side.

•Make a cardigan from a pullover by slitting open the center front of the pullover. Turn up raw edge 1/2 inch to right side. Place one-inch wide satin ribbon along the edge and topstitch in place. Voila—you've hemmed and trimmed your sweater in one step.

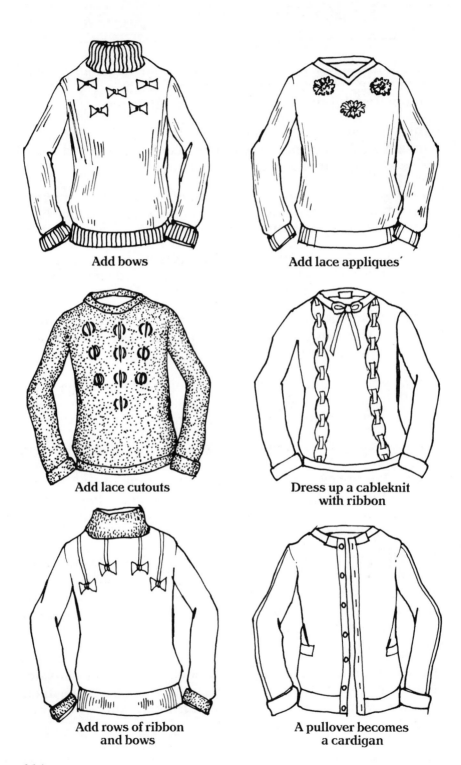

Add bows

Add lace appliqués´

Add lace cutouts

Dress up a cableknit
with ribbon

Add rows of ribbon
and bows

A pullover becomes
a cardigan

VERY IMPORTANT VEST

A vest, fashion experts inform us, is a shortcut to a two-piece suit, particularly during the warm summer months. If a skirt requires one yard of 60-inch fabric, a vest will require only an additional $1/2$ to $5/8$ yards of fabric plus lining.

Using the ready-to-wear technique described below, a vest can be completely machine sewn. An added advantage is it will never again be necessary to match shoulder seams only to discover the back to be half an inch wider than the front.

Instructions may seem confusing at first reading, but keep them at hand as you follow each step. (I always do.)

•Cut lining and vest identically. If the vest pattern has a hem allowance, trim this allowance to ⁵/₈ inch.

•Stitch any darts or princess seams in lining and vest so that the back and the fronts are complete.

•Interfacing may be done at this point. Complete any pockets, welts, or flaps now, while front is flat.

•Join fronts and back at shoulder seams—both vest and lining.

•With right sides together, stitch lining to vest at armholes. Stitch the entire front edge including hem, center, and neckline. Stitch along back hemline.

•Trim seam allowances and turn vest through shoulders.

•Use soap and ruler to mark seam allowances on wrong side of both lining and vest as the next step will be sewn "blind."

•Close one side seam of vest, stitching back to front, right sides together. Continue stitching to close lining; in essence you will be sewing in a circle. For easy access, pull the area to be seamed through opposite side seam.

•Close the remaining side seam in a similar manner, but leave a five-inch opening at the center of the lining seam. Turn vest right side out. Before closing lining side seam, press side seams open.

•Close lining seam with topstitching. This seam is the giveaway: next time you're shopping fine ready-to-wear, check the inside seam of a vest. You'll probably see the lining seam was closed with topstitching, indicating the above construction method was used. (I confess I seldom bother closing this seam as it presses flat and seems to disappear.)

•To finish vest, smooth lining to inside, and pin edges flat. Secure lining and at the same time add detail by topstitching around edges. For a dressy look, use only one row of topstitching; for a more casual look, add a second row of topstitching.

QUICK QUILTEDS

Quilted coats and vests are both fashionable and practical: they are good-looking and stylish, warm, yet lightweight. For home seamstresses, the great news is many of the pre-quilted fabrics used in fine ready-to-wear are available through fabric stores.

The coat and vest pictured were made from just two yards of a 42-inch wide channel quilted. A double-face quilted means no lining, facings, or interfacings. Expenses are cut of course, but the real bonus is the time saved in making a coat from only one thickness of fabric.

Photograph Courtesy of Cincinnati Enquirer

Quilteds, too, mean creative sewing because of the many different options in seaming, trims, and closures:

•Add color and design interest with the addition of ribbed trim on cuffs, collar, or as pictured, on pockets. Piping, brightly colored jumbo zippers, toggles, and embroidered trims might be used as well.

•Shop for unique trim ideas in ready-to-wear. Watch for the clever use of foldover braid, for example, in finishing edges.

•The channel quilted I used is vertically quilted and was used on the little girl's parka. For the boy's vest, however, the pattern was placed crosswise so quilting is horizontal.

SEWING FUNDAMENTALS
•Cut quilteds single thickness, being certain to flip pattern pieces to avoid ending up with two left sleeves or a similar disaster. The real watchword in cutting, is planning. It is important that channels are uniformly centered on the fronts and back and match at the shoulders, particularly when using quilted with wide channels.

•A vest is a breeze if the side seams are eliminated by matching seamlines and joining the front and back pattern pieces together for a seamless one-piece garment. If quilting runs horizontally around the vest, it's important to place hem at a point leaving a full channel.

•Ignore any initial inclination to cut away the lofty fiberfill in order to reduce bulk in the seams. Instead, push the fiberfill away from the seam areas and pin together the two fabric layers about one inch from the seamlines. Stitch seams conventionally. Then choose a finish from the following alternatives:

•Trim seam allowances to 1/4 inch and finish with a three-step zigzag stitch, or

•Stitch seam a second time about 1/4 inch from the first row of stitching, using either a straight stitch or zigzag stitch. Trim away seam allowances close to stitching, or

•Seam and overcast in one step if your machine is equipped with such a feature.

PIPING EDGES
Piping can add color, strengthen seams, and furnish a quick edge finish. The technique below is great for the armholes of a vest, for cuffs, and hems:

•For ease in handling, apply piping while a sleeve is flat, or before closing the shoulder seam of a one-piece vest. For a vest having side seams as well as shoulder seams, close shoulder seams, apply piping, then close side seams.

•This technique requires only quarter inch seam allowances, so trim seams accordingly. Place piping on right side of the lining layer. Align raw edges and machine stitch, keeping stitches close to stitches on piping.

•Push fiberfill away from piped edge and pin the two layers of fabric together.

•Working with garment right side out, fold under the raw edge of the outer layer and pin so both layers neatly abut the piping. Using a zipper foot, topstitch close to edge of outer layer.

ZIPPER
A zipper is handled using basically the same principle applied in attaching the piping:

•Place zipper face up on the right side of the lining layer. Position edge of zipper tape about $3/8$ inch from fabric edge. Machine stitch from zipper base with zipper tape next to needle. Machine stitching should be $1/4$ inch from zipper tape edge.

Right side
of outer layers

Stitch piping to right side
of lining layer; fold seam
allowance to inside.

Then topstitch along edge
of outer layer.

•Push fiberfill away from zipper area and pin fabric layers together. Turn seam allowance toward inside of jacket. Fold under the raw edge of the outer layer of fabric and pin to zipper tape. What you now have is a zipper sandwich.

•Topstitch close to edge on outer layer, again stitching from bottom to top.

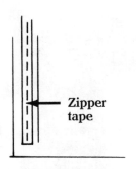

Zipper tape

Stitch zipper tape
to right side of
lining layer.

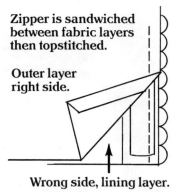

Zipper is sandwiched
between fabric layers
then topstitched.

Outer layer
right side.

Wrong side, lining layer.

CARE AND FEEDING
OF A SEWING MACHINE

If you have access to an experienced sewing machine repair-
man, consider yourself fortunate. I do! Bob Kramer and his
father are Viking dealers in Cincinnati. The two men have a
combined total of sixty years experience in the sewing machine business.

They say 80% of the service calls they receive could have been avoided if proper care had been given the ailing machine. Proper care, Bob Kramer says, involves four basics: changing needles, cleaning, oiling (though some new models such as Viking, require no lubricants) and correct usage of the machine.

NEEDLES
Change needles frequently. Needles should be changed as frequently as after the completion of every other garment. Needles dull easily and a dull needle will damage both fabric and machine. Buy good quality needles such as Schmetz.

Use the correct size and type of needle to coordinate with the thread and fabric you use. Ball point needles are necessary when sewing knit fabrics; fine needles (size 9 or 11) are required for sewing thin, tightly woven fabrics. A larger needle is needed for buttonhole twist and other heavy threads. Sometimes a needle may become sticky. If you are in the midst of a sticky situation, when using double face tape, for example, remove the sticky residue with alcohol.

Bob says often a "broken" machine brought in for service has an improperly inserted needle.

CLEANING
Remove throat plate and use a small brush to clean bobbin case assembly and under feed dogs whenever lint begins to accumulate. (I carefully vacuum the bobbin case area with a narrow sweeper attachment.)

Use a thin strip of cloth to wipe between tension discs. Keep shuttle post (the peg on which bobbin case hangs) clean of lint and thread.

OILING
Remember to keep your machine lubricated. Use a pure oil containing no detergents. It's best to buy oil manufactured for sewing machine use. Multipurpose oils may eventually cause mechanisms to lock. Oil your machine about every other month or after every 15 hours of sewing. Use only one drop in each designated oil spot.

After oiling, run machine for a short period with presser foot raised and without thread or fabric. Allow machine to rest, then sew on a fabric scrap to check for excess oil. It may be necessary to wipe excess oil from needle and needle bar.

CORRECT USAGE

Thread machine properly, making certain upper thread is situated between the tension discs. Be sure bobbin is wound evenly and bobbin case is threaded and inserted correctly. "Correctly" means when bobbin is inserted in its case and facing you, the bobbin will move clockwise when thread is pulled.

Though your machine will probably sew even when the bobbin is inserted backwards, basic machine technology dictates the machine will run more quietly and smoothly when the bobbin has been correctly inserted.

Begin sewing with take-up lever at its highest position. Always hold threads to the side or rear to prevent tangling and to insure proper tension on the very first stitch. This will also prevent the needle from pounding the fabric edge into the needle hole. At the end of a seam, do not raise the presser bar until the take-up lever is at its highest position.

Avoid adjusting the bobbin tension. Bobbin tension is very sensitive and should be adjusted only as a last resort.

Skipped stitches, Bob says, are one of the most frequent complaints he encounters. Here are some probable causes:

•**Needle of inferior quality, even when new.** The needle may be dull or bent. It may have been placed incorrectly in the needle clamp or you may have chosen the wrong needle for the fabric or thread you are using. Use the thinnest needle possible for your thread and fabric.

•**Poor quality thread.** Use a good quality thread such as Coats and Clark. Some inexpensive poly threads are too stiff and coarse, making loop formation difficult or impossible. Be sure the machine is threaded correctly.

124

•**Insufficient presser foot pressure.** If presser foot pressure is insufficient to hold fabric tautly over needle plate hole, the fabric will be pulled up and down during stitching. Try increasing foot pressure. Make certain you're not using a zipper foot or buttonhole foot for ordinary stitching.

•**Excess fabric finish.** A heavy fabric finish will deter stitch formation. Pre-laundering will eliminate this problem. Apply tension to fabric from both front and back as fabric passes under needle.

O! CHRISTMAS TREE!

Sometime around December 15 each year, I find myself imagining it would be great fun to make some gifts and holiday decorations, fully realizing, of course, those projects might still be unfinished and gathering dust on Valentine's Day.

Sound familiar? The festive stuffed tree pictured, might be just the inspiration you need to get an early start on the holidays this year. Incidentally, this item drew more reader response than any other article I have written.

Photograph Courtesy of Cincinnati Enquirer

These trees were the focal point of a holiday decorating theme in Cincinnati's most exclusive department store. Shoppers could purchase a medium-sized tree for about $35 or a somewhat larger version for $50. But you, dear reader, if you have a sewing machine and a few hours to spare, can make a tree for about $5 to $6.

You'll need 1 1/2 yards of 45-inch woven fabric. Though I used a strawberry print, holiday prints or calico are excellent alternatives. You'll also need 1 1/2 one-pound bags of poly fiberfill.

CUTTING
Using the pattern found at the back of this book, cut six whole tree shapes from fabric of your choice.

SEWING
•With right sides together, stitch two trees together, stitching about 1/4 inch from the edge. Stitch around the entire tree, stopping five inches short of the center on either side of the base. Fiberfill will later be inserted through this opening. Stitch together three pairs of tree shapes.

•Trim seam allowances at points and clip notches on curves and angles so edges will be smooth. Turn all three trees right side out. Smooth points and press edges flat.

•Keeping stitching as close to edge as possible, topstitch around entire edge of each tree (remembering to leave an opening at the base). Don't skip topstitching. Topstitching will give a clean, sharp edge to the finished tree shape.

•Place the three completed tree shapes one on top of the other. Smooth and pin fabric so there are no wrinkles. Stitch down the entire center of the trees from top to base.

STUFFING
•Begin by stuffing the points, and finally the centers of each of the six segments. Stuff with small pieces of fiberfill, taking care not to pack stuffing too tightly. (My little boy was four years old when I first made this tree and he did a great job stuffing.)

Stack three trees one on top of the other. Stitch down center.

•When stuffing is completed, close the base openings with hand stitching.

TRIMMING
The finished tree might be further decorated with tiny ornaments, satin bows, tiny pieces of fruit, hearts, miniature golf or tennis balls or any other trim you desire.

Another variation is to stitch rickrack into the seamlines of three trees before joining the second layer of fabric. The addition of rickrack will eliminate the need for topstitching around the entire edge of each tree shape.

HOME-GROWN SEWING AIDS

Special scissors for cutting $30-a-yard silk...a sewing machine costing over $1,000...ten special tools just for pressing...suddenly sewing begins to sound like a pastime for the affluent.

On the other hand, a bit of ingenuity plus a few odds and ends can produce several indispensable sewing and pressing aids. The money you save can go towards things more fun than a needle board or thread caddy.

SEAM ROLL
Make a seam roll instead of buying one for $10. Stack two or three magazines the size of Vogue or Good Housekeeping. Beginning at the bound edge, roll the magazines tightly to make a cylinder 2½ to 3 inches across. Secure with masking tape.

To cover the "seam roll", cut a 17 x 36 inch rectangle from an old sheet, tablecloth, or similar cotton remnant. Fold to measure 17 x 18 inches.

No sewing is necessary; simply place seam roll at the cut edges and roll towards remnant fold. (See diagram.) Tuck ends into roll.

What to do with a seam roll? Place the seam roll inside a sleeve while pressing open a seam. This gadget will eliminate unsightly creases on sleeves that occur in pressing.

PANTS PRESSING BOARD

Next time you're in a fabric store, ask for an empty bolt board (the cardboard on which fabric is rolled and displayed). The clerks will gladly accommadate you by pulling a discarded bolt board from the trash. Slip the bolt board inside a pants leg to press open seams without pressing in wrinkles on the under layer of fabric.

THREAD CADDY

If you have fifty spools of thread piled in a shoe box, make a thread caddy to store thread in an orderly fashion. Begin with a wood scrap, say 6 x 15 inches, or cut to your specifications. Hammer headless nails in a staggered pattern about 1 3/4 inches apart. Hang thread caddy board above sewing table.

FABRIC MARKER

My favorite home-grown sewing aid is a tiny sliver of bath soap for marking fabric. Soap makes a sharp, fine, easy-to-see line like no other tailor's chalk. The soap line remains visible in handling, yet steams away without a trace.

Keep slivers of several brands and colors on hand. One sliver may work well on wool, while another sliver marks best on synthetics. When a sliver becomes dull, use it to wash your hands and to make the sliver sharp again. Caution: Complextion soaps with lotion may leave a greasy line that won't wash out of a dark color poly silky.

TAILOR'S HAM
Instead of paying $9 to $12 for a tailor's ham, you can make one by stitching together ham-shaped layers of wool and denim. Stuff the ham-shaped layers with fiberfill, or better still, saw dust.

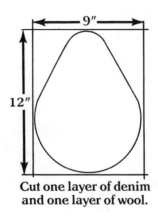

**Cut one layer of denim
and one layer of wool.**

Easiest and cheapest tailor ham in existence—use a child's stuffed toy to support curved seams when pressing.

NEEDLEBOARD
A needleboard is a pressing surface covered with bristle-like projections. Corduroy or velvet, which tends to flatten in pressing, is placed face down on the bristles. When pressed from the wrong side, the pile will not flatten. A needleboard is great to have, but costs about $25.

There's absolutely no need to spend more on tools than fabric! A fluffy terry towel will provide an excellent substitute for a needleboard when pressing napped fabric. A piece of the same fabric works well, too. For example, place a heavy corduroy remnant on your ironing board before pressing a corduroy garment. Place fabrics right sides together and press on the wrong side.

This method works so well that I have fused interfacing to velveteen using a velveteen scrap on the ironing board. Amazingly, the face of the velveteen fabric remained unmarred.

CLASSY COATS

Who has time to make a winter coat? You do—if you make a coat such as the one pictured. This coat is unstructured and uses special sewing techniques which lend style but, nevertheless, are time savers.

Trimmed in Ultrasuede®, the luxurious, lofty mohair is warm, even without a lining, as are the beautiful double face coatings available where fine fabrics are sold.

Photograph Courtesy of Cincinnati Enquirer

Though such fabrics may cost $30 to $50 per yard, the cost of the fabric is more than offset by the time and dollars saved by the elimination of interfacing, lining, and extra coating for facings and double thickness collars.

While Ultrasuede® is hardly bargain priced, only one-fourth yard of Ultrasuede® was used and absolutely no other treatment could have worked so effectively.

PATTERN
Choose a pattern with simple lines: straight sides, shawl collar, and dropped shoulders—perfect for topping blazers and suits.

SEAMS
Since there is no lining, seams must be attractive outside and inside as well. The pattern this coat is based upon suggested binding seams and edges with nylon braid—a treatment definitely not suitable for a luxurious mohair.

Ultrasuede® trim seemed a far better choice, although a good quality wool braid (if one can be found) might be a good choice also.

This sewing project presents something of an engineering challenge. My original intention was to use flat felled side seams, then to cover the shoulder, arm, and collar seams with Ultrasuede, and finally, to finish the collar and center front edges by sandwiching the mohair between two strips of Ultrasuede.®

Mohair, I discovered, is a bit bulky for flat felled seams, but through trial and error I found another method that worked quite satisfactorily: Stitch conventional ⁵/₈ inch seams; trim one seam allowance to ¹/₄ inch. Press the untrimmed seam allowance over the trimmed allowance, and topstitch on the right side.

SHOULDER AND COLLAR SEAMS
Stitch conventional ⁵/₈ inch seams, but with wrong sides together and seam allowances on outside. Stitch seams a second time about ¹/₄ inch from first stitching. Trim seam allowance

close to second row of stitching. Press seam allowances flat toward coat front.

Cut strips of Ultrasuede® ⁵/₈ inch wide (experimentation proved this to be the most attractive width). To keep bulk from seams, allow only ¹/₈ inch allowance at each end of strip.

Center Ultrasuede® strips on shoulder seam. Without prior pinning, taping, or fusing, topstitch Ultrasuede® strips to coat. Topstitch along edges with care, keeping stitches well away from edge. Viking's teflon coated machine foot will cut friction and allow machine to feed smoothly.

The collar is applied using this same method. Press seam allowance up toward collar.

NECK/CENTER FRONT EDGES AND CUFFS
Beginning with the cuffs, I tried (and tried) to sandwich the mohair between two strips of Ultrasuede.® My efforts succeeded, finally, but an excellent alternative method evolved, which worked beautifully on the center front and collar:

Fold to right side, pin, and machine baste the ⁵/₈ inch seam allowance along the center fronts and collar edges. (See diagram.) Cover seam allowance with a strip of Ultrasuede® topstitched to the right side. To do this properly, keep in mind:

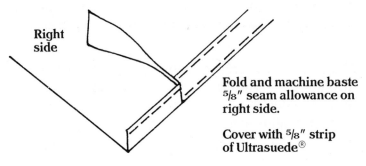

Right side

Fold and machine baste ⁵/₈" seam allowance on right side.

Cover with ⁵/₈" strip of Ultrasuede®

•Strips will be topstitched along each edge, stitching in the same direction each time. The pressure of the presser foot will cause Ultrasuede® to stretch during stitching. Upon relaxing, it will draw up, creating ripples. Presser foot pressure, therefore, must be very light.

•Baste Ultrasuede® with fusible web or glue stick.

•Stitch Ultrasuede® strips to front and collar in two separate units, beginning at the hem and finishing at center back of collar.

CLOSURES
Choose from a variety of closures or create your own design:

•Sew patches of Ultrasuede® on right front to accommodate buttonholes. On the left side, back buttons with smaller buttons.

•Stitch a casing of purchased satin bias tape to inside. Casing might stop at side seams or near center front. Tie with a belt of coating fabric or Ultrasuede®.

•Make Ultrasuede® loops to button Ultrasuede®-covered buttons.

CHEERFUL CHILD SEWING TIPS

HELP!
My jeans
are falling
down

BUS
STOP

Study a group of children at play and attempt to figure out which child's mother has been busy sewing. Over there, a little boy wearing a crew neck tee shirt is whining, "I hate this dumb shirt." It's pink and yellow striped and the stripes are four inches wide. (His mother sews.)

She should be reminded pink and yellow fabric is for a feminine garment and that small garments call for scaled down stripes and prints.

Another little boy is wearing jeans and his favorite shirt. No mother in her right mind sews jeans, but his mother did sew the shirt. Qualify that statement: mothers in their right minds do sew jeans, but it takes a tremendous amount of time. His white knit V-neck shirt has a navy collar and red ribbing.

Both mothers spent approximately the same amount of time in sewing; the difference was in the planning. It took no more time to use contrasting fabrics. Nor was cost a factor because leftover scraps were used.

In sewing, details generally take more thought than sewing time or money. In the long run, it pays to produce a child's favorite garment rather than one that will hang in the closet till it's outgrown.

WHEN FITTING IS THE PITS

Whether sewing for children or just finding properly fitted ready-to-wear, fitting can present problems. Jeans, for example, require so many fitting checkpoints: the waist, crotch length, hem length, not to mention satisfying a child with the right fabric, color, number of pockets and design detail. Whew! Sometimes it's tough being a mother.

Should you, by some remote chance, find a pair of jeans correct in color, length and number of pockets, but too big around the waist—grab them. Ten minutes worth of sewing will correct the problem:

•On the inside layer only of the waistband, cut a half-inch opening. Cut a second similar opening at the other end of the waistband. (See diagram.) Measure the distance between the two slits.

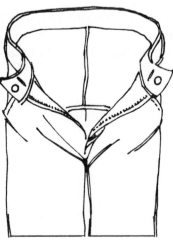

Cut ¹/₂″ slits at ends on inside layer of waistband.

•Cut a length of 3/4-inch elastic one inch smaller than the distance between the two slits. Pull elastic through waistband between slits.

•Use a zigzag stitch to secure one end of the elastic, stitching through elastic and both thicknesses of the waistband at the same time.

•With elastic pulled through remaining opening, draw up slightly. While child is wearing pants, adjust and pin elastic for a snug waistline fit.

•With elastic pinned in proper position, remove garment. Zigzag through elastic and both thicknesses of waistband. Trim excess elastic. Never again will that child bemoan the time he was climbing on the school bus and his jeans fell down!

MENDING
The sleeve seams of a jacket are subject to much stress when worn and are usually first to need repair. A completely lined jacket makes it difficult to reach inside seams and few of us can bear to rip open a perfectly good seam just for the privilege of mending it.

Not to worry. Simply cut a neat, straight slash in the center back lining, close to the waist area where there is less stress than in shoulder area.

This slash will afford a convenient entry to the inside seams. After repairing seams, fold raw edges of lining inside. Pin folded edges together and close with a zigzag stitch.

NOTES

NOTES